Principles and Proverbs from Pride and Prejudice

A 120-day devotional inspired by the classic novel by Jane Austen

Chrisann Dawson

Visit Shine-A-Light Press on our website:
www.ShineALightPress.com
on Twitter: @SALPress

Visit Chrisann Dawson on her website:
www.chrisanndawson.com
on Twitter: @chrisanndawson
And on Facebook: www.facebook.com/chrisann.dawson.1

The Shine-A-Light Press logo is a trademark of Shine-A-Light Corp.

Principles and Proverbs from Pride and Prejudice
Copyright © 2020 by Chrisann Dawson

Second edition printed January, 2021 by Shine-A-Light Press in Prescott, Arizona

Second edition edited by Chris and Andrea Elston

Interior and exterior design and layout by Chris Elston

All rights reserved. Published by Shine-A-Light Press. Shine-A-Light Press and associated logos are trademarks and/or are registered trademarks of Shine-A-Light Corp. No part of this publication may be reproduced, stored in a retrieval system, or transmitted in any form or by any means, electronic, mechanical, photocopying, recording, or otherwise without written permission of Shine-A-Light Corp. For information regarding permission, please contact the permissions department at www.shinealightcorp.com.

Publisher's Note: Pride and Prejudice by Jane Austen is in the public domain. Format, type, composition, and design of this book are the exclusive property of Shine-A-Light Press. No part of this book may be used or reproduced in any manner without written permission from the publisher.

"Scripture quotations are from The ESV® Bible (The Holy Bible, English Standard Version®), copyright © 2001 by Crossway, a publishing ministry of Good News Publishers. Used by permission. All rights reserved."

ISBN 978-0-9976722-8-2

Printed in the U.S.A
U.S.A. $16.99

To Jane Austen lovers everywhere who appreciate her insights into relationships.

ACKNOWLEDGMENTS

I would like to acknowledge the influence of both God's Word and the classical writings of Jane Austen on my personal life. Both have contributed to my personal growth and confidence.

I would also like to thank my first edition editors, Susan Cordaro, Jim Hurlburt, Margot Tan, and Amy VanZile.

Finally, I'd like to thank Shine-A-Light Press for their affirmation and professionalism.

Principles and Proverbs from Pride and Prejudice

Chrisann Dawson

DAY ONE

"It is a truth universally acknowledged, that a single man in possession of a good fortune, must be in want of a wife. However little known the feelings or views of such a man may be on his first entering the neighborhood, this truth is so well fixed in the minds of the surrounding families, that he is considered as the rightful property of some one or other of their daughters."

He who finds a wife finds a good thing...
Proverbs 18:22

※

Pride and Prejudice opens with this beautiful line that declares that all single, rich young men must be in search of the perfect partner to share their lives and fortunes with. Scripture supports the idea that a good wife is a treasure, worth the seeking and prized when found. The word "finds" implies acquiring after a diligent search. We are worth being sought after. We are valuable, a treasure.

DAY TWO

❦

"Do not *you* want to know who has taken it?" cried his wife impatiently.

"You want to tell me, and I have no objection to hearing it."

That was invitation enough.

Love is patient and kind...
1 Corinthians 13:4

❧

Mrs. Bennet, the mother of five grown daughters, wants to engage her husband in a conversation about this new single man. She does so, referring to a neighboring mansion. Mrs. Bennet lived for only one goal: to see her daughters all happily married to rich, young men with the means to be able to care for them properly.

Longbourn, the Bennet family's estate, came to Mr. Bennet through an entail. If a property was entailed, it could only pass to male heirs. Mr. and Mrs. Bennet's original plan was to have a son, keep the estate in the family, and provide for Mrs. Bennet and daughters, but no son arrived; only five daughters. The girls' only hope for being cared for financially was marrying someone with money.

Mrs. Bennet's pursuit of husbands for her daughters often motivated her to act foolishly and annoyingly. Patience was often the necessary ingredient for Mr. Bennet to endure his wife's folly. After more than twenty years of marriage, he had learned to patiently tolerate his wife's foolishness.

Practicing patience, tolerance, and kindness is vital to any relationship, especially marriage.

DAY THREE

❧❦

"Oh! single, my dear, to be sure! A single man of large fortune; four or five thousand a year. What a fine thing for our girls!"

"How so? How can it affect them?"

"My dear Mr. Bennet," replied his wife, "how can you be so tiresome! You must know that I am thinking of his marrying one of them."

"Is that his design in settling here?"

"Design! nonsense, how can you talk so! But it is very likely that he may fall in love with one of them, and therefore you must visit him as soon as he comes."

"I see no occasion for that. You and the girls may go, or you may send them by themselves, which perhaps will be still better, for as you are as handsome as any of them, Mr. Bingley may like you the best of the party."

Do not toil to acquire wealth;
be discerning enough to desist.
Proverbs 23:4

Mr. Bennet's toying with his wife was a game he often played. The custom of the day insisted that introductions be formal. As the head of his home, Mr. Bennet was expected to pay a visit to Mr. Bingley before any of the rest of the family would have a chance to get to know him. Mr. Bennet was the key to one of his daughters marrying this new young neighbor; as he well knew; and he thoroughly enjoyed the idea of pretending that he would not pay the visit.

Often other people in our lives attempt to steer our direction and decision-making with their goals for our lives. Scheming ways to become rich, especially through marriage, contradicts Biblical principles, and often leads to misery. Neither Mr. Bennet, nor Mrs. Bennet take seriously the role they are playing in the lives of their daughters.

DAY FOUR

❧❦

"My dear, you flatter me. I certainly *have* had my share of beauty, but I do not pretend to be anything extraordinary now. When a woman has five grown-up daughters, she ought to give over thinking of her own beauty."

"In such cases, a woman has not often much beauty to think of."

*Charm is deceitful, and beauty is vain, but a
woman who fears the Lord is to be praised.*
Proverbs 31:30

Self-absorption will diminish any true beauty. Mrs. Bennet, although claiming to only think of her daughters and their need for rich husbands, primarily thought only of herself. Wisdom and proper speaking would have only enhanced any lingering beauty that Mrs. Bennet possessed. Let us be different from this self-centered mother. Let us appreciate ourselves; care for our body but focus principally on nurturing our internal beauty through a strong relationship with God.

DAY FIVE

❧❧

"I dare say Mr. Bingley will be very glad to see you; and I will send a few lines by you to assure him of my hearty consent to his marrying whichever he chooses of the girls; though I must throw in a good word for my little Lizzy."

"I desire you will do no such thing. Lizzy is not a bit better than the others; and I am sure she is not half so handsome as Jane, nor half so good-humored as Lydia. But you are always giving her the preference."

"They have none of them much to recommend them," replied he; "they are all silly and ignorant like other girls; but Lizzy has something more of quickness than her sisters."

"Mr. Bennet, how can you abuse your own children in such a way?"

Buy truth, and do not sell it; buy wisdom, instruction, and understanding.
Proverbs 23:23

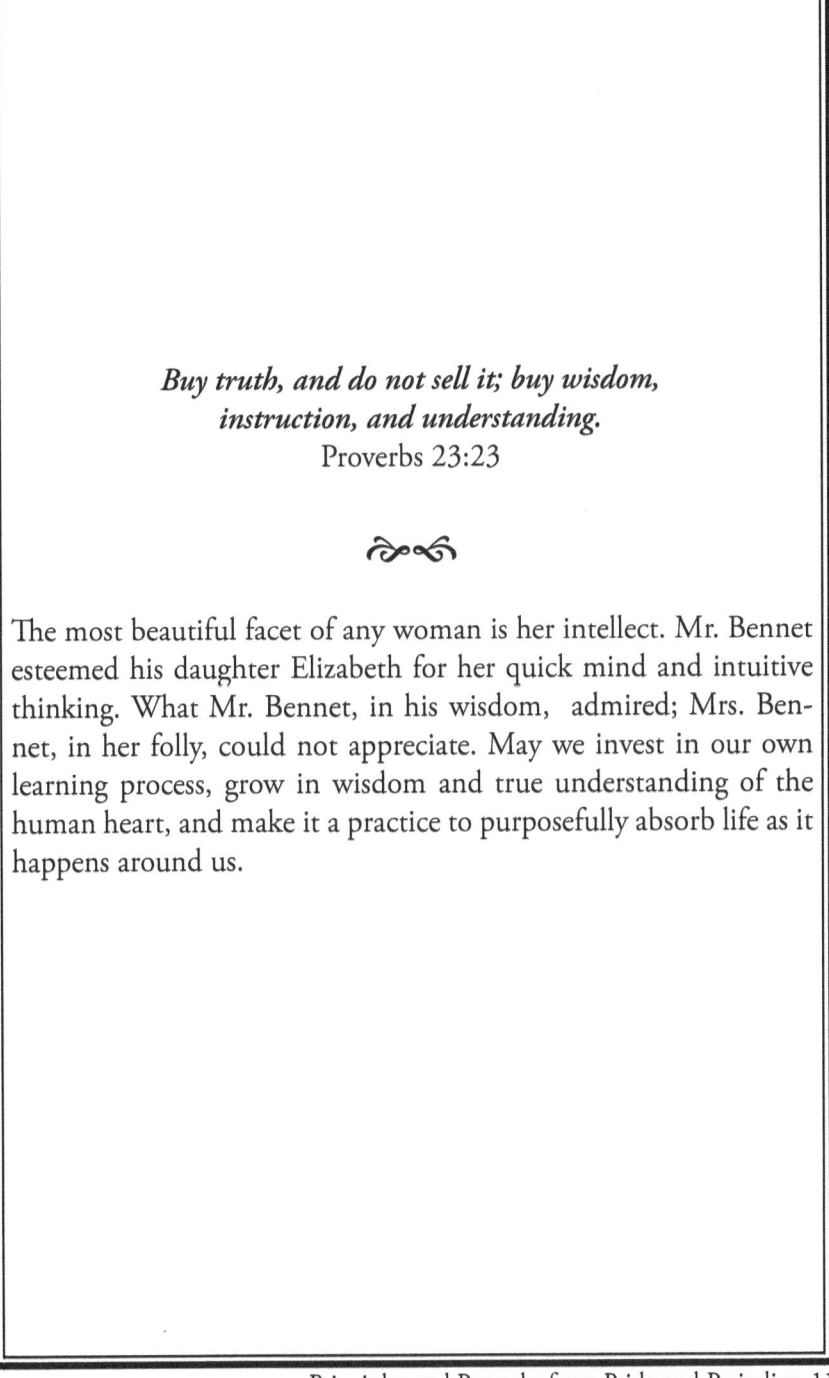

The most beautiful facet of any woman is her intellect. Mr. Bennet esteemed his daughter Elizabeth for her quick mind and intuitive thinking. What Mr. Bennet, in his wisdom, admired; Mrs. Bennet, in her folly, could not appreciate. May we invest in our own learning process, grow in wisdom and true understanding of the human heart, and make it a practice to purposefully absorb life as it happens around us.

DAY SIX

❧

"Mr. Bennet, how can you abuse your own children in such a way? You take delight in vexing me. You have no compassion for my poor nerves."

"You mistake me, my dear. I have a high respect for your nerves. They are my old friends. I have heard you mention them with consideration these last twenty years at least."

"Ah, you do not know what I suffer."

"But I hope you will get over it, and live to see many young men of four thousand a year come into the neighborhood."

"It will be no use to us, if twenty such should come, since you will not visit them."

"Depend upon it, my dear, that when there are twenty, I will visit them all."

*Whoever covers an offense seeks love, but he who
repeats a matter separates close friends.*
Proverbs 17:9

☙❧

Mr. Bennet has practiced "covering his wife's transgressions" for their more than twenty years of marriage together. This is a two-sided coin: may we not be the irritating one, whose transgressions require a covering; that needs to be tolerated. May we practice, through seeking love, being the one tolerant of other people's weaknesses.

DAY SEVEN

❧

When she was discontented, she fancied herself nervous. The business of her life was to get her daughters married; its solace was visiting and news.

. . . a whisperer separates close friends.
Proverbs 16:28

(Mr. Bennet was among the earliest of those who waited on Mr. Bingley. He had always intended to visit him, though to the last always assuring his wife that he should not go; and till the evening after the visit was paid, she had no knowledge of it.)

Mrs. Bennet made a habit of comforting herself by seeking the latest "news" or gossip while visiting her friends. It is said that a weak mind speaks of people; an average mind speaks of events; a strong mind speaks of ideas. The sad state of the marriage of Mr. and Mrs. Bennet has primarily evolved as a direct result of the foolishness of Mrs. Bennet, and her willingness to share her lack of wisdom with anyone who will listen. May we become a thoughtful and wise speaker.

DAY EIGHT

※

Mr. Bennet was among the earliest of those who waited on Mr. Bingley. He had always intended to visit him, though to the last always assuring his wife that he should not go; and till the evening after the visit was paid she had no knowledge of it. It was then disclosed in the following manner. Observing his second daughter employed in trimming a hat, he suddenly addressed her with,

"I hope Mr. Bingley will like it, Lizzy."

"We are not in a way to know *what* Mr. Bingley likes," said her mother resentfully, "since we are not to visit."

"But you forget, mamma," said Elizabeth, "that we shall meet him at the assemblies, and that Mrs. Long promised to introduce him."

"I do not believe Mrs. Long will do any such thing. She has two nieces of her own. She is a selfish, hypocritical woman, and I have no opinion of her."

*You have set our iniquities before you,
our secret sins in the light of your presence.*
Psalm 90:8

☙❧

Mrs. Bennet loves to gossip. Everyone knows it except her. Blind to her own folly and bad habits, Mrs. Bennet is quick to criticize in others what is most evident in her own life. Since our true self is open to God (and usually before others), let us be transparent ABOUT ourselves TO ourselves.

DAY NINE

❦

The girls stared at their father. Mrs. Bennet said only, "Nonsense, nonsense!"

"What can be the meaning of that emphatic exclamation?" cried he. "Do you consider the forms of introduction, and the stress that is laid on them, as nonsense? I cannot quite agree with you there. What say you, Mary? For you are a young lady of deep reflection, I know, and read great books and make extracts."

Mary wished to say something very sensible, but knew not how.

"While Mary is adjusting her ideas," he continued, "let us return to Mr. Bingley."

"I am sick of Mr. Bingley," cried his wife.

"I am sorry to hear *that*; but why did not you tell me that before? If I had known as much this morning I certainly would not have called on him. It is very unlucky; but as I have actually paid the visit, we cannot escape the acquaintance now."

*Let the wise hear and increase in learning, and the
one who understands obtain guidance...*
Proverbs 1:5

☙❧

In his delight in teasing the foolishness of his wife, Mr. Bennet occasionally turned his wry sense of humor on one of his daughters. This time Mary received his wit. Mary, a typical middle child, always sought the approval of others. She did this through extensive reading, not with the goal to improve herself practically, but to impress her listeners. Wisdom is the motive for learning, which should be applied to our daily lives.

DAY TEN

❧❧

"How good it was in you, my dear Mr. Bennet! But I knew I should persuade you at last. I was sure you loved your girls too well to neglect such an acquaintance. Well, how pleased I am! and it is such a good joke, too, that you should have gone this morning and never said a word about it till now."

If a wise man has an argument with a fool, the fool only rages and laughs, and there is no quiet.
Proverbs 29:9

❦

Just a moment earlier, Mrs. Bennet was angry with her husband for not visiting Mr. Bingley, then was quickly overjoyed by hearing that he had already made the visit. Mr. Bennet is wise but made a foolish decision in marrying his wife. Truly, Mrs. Bennet gives her family no rest from her folly and simple-minded comments. Avoid being easily swayed from one emotion to another…avoid being a fool.

DAY ELEVEN

A few weeks later at the first assembly dance that Mr. Bingley attended with his guests, he was declared to be good looking and gentlemanlike...but his friend Mr. Darcy soon drew the attention of the room by his fine, tall person, handsome features, and his noble mien. The report in general circulation within five minutes was...of his having ten thousand a year. He was admired till his manners gave a disgust, which turned his popularity. For he was discovered to be proud...and above being pleased. Not all his large estate in Derbyshire could then save him from having the most forbidding, disagreeable countenance, and being unworthy of being compared to his friend.

*Pride goes before destruction, and a
haughty spirit before a fall.*
Proverbs 16:18

❧☙

Mr. Bingley was of average good looks and pleasant manners, but his friend, Mr. Darcy, was exceedingly handsome and very rich. For several minutes at the dance Mr. Darcy was admired by all, but quickly his proud manners made him despised. Mr. Darcy could benefit from pondering this old proverb: "Beauty is as beauty does." Mr. Darcy could improve his popularity by realizing that looking amazing and acting awful is not attractive.

DAY TWELVE

❧

"Come, Darcy," said he, "I must have you dance. I hate to see you standing about by yourself in this stupid manner. You had much better dance."

"I certainly shall not. You know how I detest it, unless I am particularly acquainted with my partner. At such an assembly as this it would be insupportable. Your sisters are engaged, and there is not another woman in the room whom it would not be a punishment to me to stand up with."

"I would not be so fastidious as you are," cried Mr. Bingley, "for a kingdom! Upon my honor, I never met with so many pleasant girls in my life as I have this evening; and there are several of them you see uncommonly pretty."

"You are dancing with the only handsome girl in the room," said Mr. Darcy, looking at the eldest Miss Bennet.

"Oh! She is the most beautiful creature I ever beheld! But there is one of her sisters sitting down just behind you, who is very pretty, and I dare say very agreeable. Do let me ask my partner to introduce you."

"Which do you mean?" and turning round he looked for a moment at Elizabeth, till catching her eye, he withdrew his own and coldly said: "She is tolerable, but not handsome enough to tempt me; I am in no humor at present to give consequence to young ladies who are slighted by other men."

Be kind to one another...
Ephesians 4:32

∾

Mr. Darcy offended Elizabeth Bennet on their first opportunity to meet. He displayed his disdain for people whom he considered below him in station. A man should always be kind and tenderhearted to any woman, and Elizabeth Bennet was more honorable than most, with both outward beauty and inward intelligence and spirit. Woman is the crown of God's creation and deserves respect.

DAY THIRTEEN

❧❧

Mr. Darcy walked off; and Elizabeth remained with no very cordial feelings toward him. She told the story, however, with great spirit among her friends; for she had a lively, playful disposition, which delighted in anything ridiculous.

The evening altogether passed off pleasantly to the whole family. Mrs. Bennet had seen her eldest daughter much admired by the Netherfield party. Mr. Bingley had danced with her twice, and she had been distinguished by his sisters. Jane was as much gratified by this as her mother could be, though in a quieter way. Elizabeth felt Jane's pleasure. Mary had heard herself mentioned to Miss Bingley as the most accomplished girl in the neighborhood; and Catherine and Lydia had been fortunate enough never to be without partners, which was all that they had yet learnt to care for at a ball.

. . . for the Lord will be your confidence. . .
Proverbs 3:26

☙◈❧

Jesus reminded us in Scripture that offenses will come; they are unavoidable. Although Elizabeth was initially hurt by Mr. Darcy's rude and self-centered comments, she decided to laugh it off and move on. Her internal strength and insight reveled in the funny side of that situation and laughed at Darcy's pride. If we fall short of Elizabeth Bennet's confidence, we can lean heavily upon the confidence of the LORD.

When Jane and Elizabeth were alone, the former, who had been cautious in her praise of Mr. Bingley before, expressed to her sister just how very much she admired him.

"He is just what a young man ought to be," said she, "sensible, good-humored, lively; and I never saw such happy manners! so much ease, with such perfect good breeding!"

"He is also handsome," replied Elizabeth, "which a young man ought likewise to be, if he possibly can. His character is thereby complete."

"I was very much flattered by his asking me to dance a second time. I did not expect such a compliment."

"Did not you? I did for you. But that is one great difference between us. Compliments always take you by surprise, and me never.

Let another praise you, and not your own mouth; a stranger, and not your own lips.
Proverbs 27:2

Like Jane, always let compliments surprise us. Because she had a modest spirit, Jane did not expect to be admired, but was pleased with the compliment. Elizabeth, due to a strong sense of self, was never surprised by praise, but rather expected it. Let's remember to graciously receive praise, but not to seek praise.

DAY FIFTEEN

❧❧

"Well, he certainly is very agreeable, and I give you leave to like him. You have liked many a stupider person."

"Dear Lizzy!"

"Oh! you are a great deal too apt, you know, to like people in general. You never see a fault in anybody. All the world are good and agreeable in your eyes. I never heard you speak ill of a human being in your life."

"I wish not to be hasty in censuring anyone; but I always speak what I think."

"I know you do; and it is *that* which makes the wonder. With *your* good sense, to be so honestly blind to the follies and nonsense of others! Affectation of candor is common enough--one meets with it everywhere. But to be candid without ostentation or design--to take the good of everybody's character and make it still better, and say nothing of the bad--belongs to you alone."

But the Lord said to Samuel, 'Do not look on his appearance or on the height of his stature, because I have rejected him. For the Lord sees not as man sees: man looks on the outward appearance, but the Lord looks on the heart.'
I Samuel 16:7

Jane and Elizabeth view people and circumstances from different perspectives. Jane, a bit naively hopeful, saw the good in everyone. Elizabeth, more jaded, analyzed everyone's motives. Even with these obvious differences in their characters, Elizabeth acknowledges that Jane is honestly sincere in her approval of everyone. The best way to observe life is through the eyes of the LORD. Often, we only look at the outward. God sees the heart. God truly knows if a person's heart is openly reflected in outward actions and appearances.

DAY SIXTEEN

꧁꧂

And so you like this man's sisters, too, do you? Their manners are not equal to his."

"Certainly not--at first. But they are very pleasing women when you converse with them. Miss Bingley is to live with her brother, and keep his house; and I am much mistaken if we shall not find a very charming neighbor in her."

Elizabeth listened in silence, but was not convinced; their behavior at the assembly had not been calculated to please in general; and with more quickness of observation and less pliancy of temper than her sister, and with a judgement too unassailed by any attention to herself, she was very little disposed to approve them. They were in fact very fine ladies; not deficient in good humor when they were pleased, nor in the power of making themselves agreeable when they chose it, but proud and conceited. They were rather handsome, had been educated in one of the first private seminaries in town, had a fortune of twenty thousand pounds, were in the habit of spending more than they ought, and of associating with people of rank, and were therefore in every respect entitled to think well of themselves, and meanly of others.

They were of a respectable family in the north of England; a circumstance more deeply impressed on their memories than that their brother's fortune and their own had been acquired by trade.

I have applied all these things to myself and Apollos for your benefit, brothers, that you may learn by us not to go beyond what is written, that none of you may be puffed up in favor of one against another. For who sees anything different in you? What do you have that you did not receive? If then you received it, why do you boast as if you did not receive it?
I Corinthians 4:6-7

❧❦

Like Mr. Darcy, Mr. Bingley's sisters were proud. Their conceit was not founded upon their own accomplishments. Rather their family's money was acquired through business and not "old" money. Unfounded pride leaves an unpleasant taste in the mouths of those who experience it.

DAY SEVENTEEN

Between Mr. Bingley and Mr. Darcy there was a very steady friendship, despite a great opposition of character. Bingley was endeared to Mr. Darcy for his easiness and openness of temper. On the strength of Darcy's regard Bingley had the firmest reliance, and of his judgment the highest opinion. In understanding and intelligence Darcy was the superior of the two. Bingley was by no means deficient, but Darcy was clever. Mr. Darcy was haughty, reserved, and fastidious. His manners were well-bred but not inviting. In that respect, his friend had greatly the advantage. Bingley was sure of being liked wherever he appeared; Darcy was continually giving offense.

The manner in which they spoke of their first assembly ball in Meryton followed their characteristics. Bingley had never met with pleasanter people or prettier girls in his life; everybody had been most kind and attentive. Darcy, on the other hand, had only seen a collection of people in which there was little beauty and no fashion.

***Iron sharpens iron, and one man
sharpens another.***
Proverbs 27:17

☙❧

Having a variety of friends with differing personality strengths and weaknesses can sharpen us and grant us the opportunity of sharpening others. The stark contrast in the characters of Mr. Bingley and Mr. Darcy illustrates how deep friendships can be forged in the presence of strong differences. Oddly enough, the combined personalities of the two men, would have made one perfect person.

DAY EIGHTEEN

❧❦

The Bennet's neighbors, the Lucas family, came by the next day to discuss the dance. Mrs. Bennet bragged on Jane's being asked twice to dance with Mr. Bingley. Charlotte commented with humor on Mr. Darcy's claim that Elizabeth was to be declared only just tolerable. Then the subject of Mr. Darcy's extreme pride was brought up.

"Mr. Darcy's pride," said Charlotte Lucas to Elizabeth the next day, "does not offend me so much as pride often does; there is an excuse for it. One cannot wonder that so very fine a young man, with family, fortune, everything in his favor should think highly of himself. If I may so express it, he has a right to be proud."

"That's true," Elizabeth said, "and I could easily forgive his pride, if he had not mortified mine."

Elizabeth's statement prompted Mary to moralize, "Pride is a very common failing I believe. By all that I have read, I am convinced that it is very common indeed."

Great peace have those who love your law; nothing can make them stumble.
Psalm 119:165

❦

When the course of the after-dance gossip led to Mr. Darcy's rude observation regarding Elizabeth being only "tolerable," the subject of pride was opened. Charlotte believed that Darcy had every excuse for being so proud. He had family, fortune, and good looks. Elizabeth chose to not be seriously offended by Mr. Darcy's comment. By laughing off his remark, she could quickly forgive any damage HIS pride had done to HER pride. Life is easier if we do not take ourselves too seriously.

DAY NINETEEN

The ladies of Longbourn soon visited the ladies of Netherfield, Mr. Bingley's sisters. Mr. Bingley, each time there was an opportunity, gave Jane a great deal of attention. Jane received this attention with the greatest of pleasure. It was generally evident that Bingley did admire Jane, and that Jane was yielding to the preference. Elizabeth observed Jane's pleasure easily, but since Jane "united with great strength of feeling, a composure of temper and a uniform cheerfulness of manner," her regard was not obvious to everyone.

Charlotte Lucas mentioned to Elizabeth her concern about the way Jane showed her affection to Mr. Bingley, "It is sometimes a disadvantage for a person to be so guarded. If a woman, like Jane, conceals her affection from the object of it, she may lose the opportunity of securing him. There is so much of gratitude or vanity in almost every attachment that it is not safe to leave any to itself. A slight preference is natural enough; but there are very few of us who have heart enough to be really in love without encouragement.

Bingley likes your sister undoubtedly; but he may never do more than like her, if she does not help him on."

"But she does help him on," Elizabeth defended, "as much as her nature will allow. If I can perceive her regard for him, he must be a simpleton not to discover it too."

"Only remember, Elizabeth, that he does not know Jane's disposition as you do."

Having purified your souls by your obedience to the truth for a sincere brotherly love, love one another earnestly from a pure heart...
1 Peter 1:22

True love is active and warm, not passive. Because Jane had a shy personality, she did not actively express her affection to Mr. Bingley and was at risk of losing him. Any relationship needs to be nurtured through purposeful, loving action.

DAY TWENTY

Occupied in observing Mr. Bingley's attentions to her sister, Elizabeth did not realize she was herself becoming an object of interest in the eyes of his friend, Mr. Darcy. At first Mr. Darcy had scarcely allowed her to be pretty; he had looked at her without admiration at the ball; and when they next met, he looked at her only to criticize. But no sooner had he made it clear to himself and his friends that Elizabeth had hardly a good feature in her face, he began, upon closer attention, to find that her face was rendered uncommonly intelligent by the beautiful expression of her dark eyes. He was also forced to acknowledge that though her figure's symmetry lacked form, it was light and pleasing. He was also caught by her easy playfulness. He began to wish to know more of her.

The eye is the lamp of the body. So, if your eye is healthy, your whole body will be full of light...
Matthew 6:22

☙❧

True beauty often shines from the soul through the expression of the eyes. Initially Mr. Darcy thought Elizabeth merely "tolerable." He declared that she was not "pretty enough" to tempt him to ask her to dance. But the expression of her eyes revealed her intelligence, and her playful manner was an expression of her genuine confidence. External beauty is enhanced by internal beauty: a cultivated mind and a playful spirit.

Elizabeth's sister Mary, the middle daughter, had the consequence of being the only plain one in the family. Mary worked hard for knowledge and accomplishments…always impatient for a chance to display them. Mary had neither genius nor taste and a conceited manner. Vanity had given Mary application-she practiced continuously, but vanity had also given her a pedantic air and a conceited manner. This attitude would have been offensive to anyone who had reached a higher degree of excellence than she had. Elizabeth, who was easy and unaffected, had been listened to with much more pleasure than Mary, though she played the piano half so well.

Not many of you should become teachers, my brothers, for you know that we who teach will be judged with greater strictness.
James 3:1

☙❧

Poor Mary, who lacked beauty to recommend herself, tried too hard to impress people with her knowledge and abilities. Sadly, her book learning did not lead her to true understanding of people or to wise decisions. Mary's conceit in what she assumed were her abilities caused disgust in the minds of those she sought to impress. Because Mary assumed the role of being everyone's teacher and no one's friend, Mary always fell short of her goal of impressing her audience.

DAY TWENTY-TWO

૭౿⃰ஓ

At a second assembly ball, Elizabeth turned down a request from Mr. Darcy to dance. Elizabeth's resistance had not injured her with the gentleman, and he was thinking of her with some complacency, when he was accosted by Miss Bingley.

"I can guess the subject of your reverie."

"I should imagine not."

"You are considering how insupportable it would be to pass many evenings in this manner—in such society, and indeed I am quite of your opinion. I was never more annoyed! The insipidity, and yet the noise-- the nothingness, and yet the self-importance of all those people! What would I give to hear your strictures on them!"

"Your conjecture is totally wrong, I assure you. My mind was more agreeably engaged. I have been meditating on the very great pleasure which a pair of fine eyes in the face of a pretty woman can bestow."

Miss Bingley immediately fixed her eyes on his face, and desired he would tell her what lady had the credit of inspiring such reflections. Mr. Darcy replied with great intrepidity,—

"Miss Elizabeth Bennet."

*Do not let your adorning be external—the
braiding of hair and the putting on of gold jewelry,
or the clothing you wear— but let your adorning
be the hidden person of the heart with the
imperishable beauty of a gentle and quiet spirit,
which in God's sight is very precious.*
1 Peter 3:3-4

The truth of the well-known adage, "beauty is in the eye of the beholder," is illustrated here. At first Mr. Darcy did not appreciate Elizabeth's beauty, but observing her intelligence, her playful spirit, and her strength of character, had changed his mind. Who she truly was as a person affected how she appeared in the eyes of her admirer.

DAY TWENTY-THREE

❧

Catherine and Lydia, the two younger Bennet girls, were well supplied both with news and happiness by the arrival of a militia regiment to the neighborhood, which were to winter in Meryton.

After listening one morning to their effusions on this subject, Mr. Bennet coolly observed,—

"From all that I can collect by your manner of talking, you must be two of the silliest girls in the country. I have suspected it some time, but I am now convinced."

Catherine was disconcerted, and made no answer; but Lydia, with perfect indifference, continued to express her admiration of Captain Carter, and her hope of seeing him in the course of the day, as he was going the next morning to London.

"I am astonished, my dear," said Mrs. Bennet, "that you should be so ready to think your own children silly. If I wished to think slightingly of anybody's children, it should not be of my own, however."

"If my children are silly, I must hope to be always sensible of it."

*The fear of the Lord is the beginning of knowledge;
fools despise wisdom and instruction.*
Proverbs 1:7

☙❧

Catherine and Lydia talked of nothing but officers and gossip. Their minds were continuously occupied with their own pleasures…no serious learning. Mr. Bennet, an honest but disengaged father, admitted that they were empty-headed, not a condition to emulate.

DAY TWENTY-FOUR

❧❧

AUTHOR'S SUMMARY OF EVENTS FROM PRIDE AND PREJUDICE:

When the Bingley sisters invited Jane to dine with them, Mrs. Bennet decided to send Jane on horseback, hoping she would get caught in the rain, and be forced to spend the night. Mrs. Bennet's plan worked, except that Jane came down with a violent cold by being soaked to the skin, which forced the Bingley family to give Jane a room until she recovered.

The next morning, Elizabeth decided to walk the three-mile distance, through the mud to visit Jane, who she dearly loved. Elizabeth arrived muddy but beautiful and was met with surprise by everyone in Mr. Bingley's home. That Elizabeth should have walked three miles so early in the day, in such dirty weather, and by herself, was almost incredible to Miss Bingley and Mrs. Hurst. Elizabeth felt that the sisters held her in contempt for her walking so far. Mr. Bingley received her with good humor and kindness. Mr. Darcy was "divided between admiration of the brilliancy which exercise had given to Elizabeth's complexion, and doubt as to Jane's illness justifying her coming so far alone."

Let love be genuine. Abhor what is evil;
hold fast to what is good.
Romans 12:9

Elizabeth deeply loved Jane. She did not care how a three-mile walk through mud would make her appear to Mr. Bingley and his family and friends, and they judged her exactly in the manner she had anticipated. Elizabeth's genuine love for Jane (and her love of walking) prompted her to give of her time and energy without self-thought.

DAY TWENTY-FIVE

❧❦

"Elizabeth has nothing to recommend her but being an excellent walker. I shall never forget her appearance this morning. She really looked almost wild...her petticoat six inches deep in mud...I am afraid, Mr. Darcy, that this adventure has rather affected your admiration of her fine eyes."

"Not at all," Mr. Darcy replied, "they were rather brightened by the exercise."

A dishonest man spreads strife,
and a whisperer separates close friends.
Proverbs 16:28

❦

Elizabeth was invited to stay at Netherfield, Mr. Bingley's home, while Jane was recuperating. Unlike Jane, Elizabeth did not like or trust Mr. Bingley's sisters, especially Caroline, the unmarried one. Elizabeth saw them as insincere. After leaving the dining room later in the day to return to Jane who was in poor health due to her terrible cold, Miss Bingley began 'abusing her as soon as she was out of the room.'

In an attempt to regain Mr. Darcy's attention, Caroline Bingley began to malign Elizabeth as soon as she was out of the room. Unfortunately for Caroline, her gossip had the opposite effect by reminding Mr. Darcy how beautiful Elizabeth's eyes looked after her vigorous walk. Caroline's proclivity for gossip was backfiring by separating her from Mr. Darcy's regard.

DAY TWENTY-SIX

❧❦

Elizabeth noted: "I wonder who first discovered the efficacy of poetry in driving away love!"

Mr. Darcy was surprised, "I have been used to consider poetry as the food of love."

"Of a fine, stout, healthy love it may. Everything nourishes what is strong already. But if it be only a slight, thin sort of inclination, I am convinced one good sonnet will starve it entirely away," she finished.

Darcy only smiled; and the general pause in the conversation which ensued made Elizabeth tremble lest her mother should be exposing herself again.

Many waters cannot quench love,
neither can floods drown it.
If a man offered for love
all the wealth of his house,
he would be utterly despised.
Song of Solomon 8:7

Mrs. Bennet and the younger girls spent some time with Jane in Mr. Bingley's house, assessing exactly how sick she was. Upon being assured she was satisfactorily improving, Mrs. Bennet, Catherine, and Lydia visited with Mr. Bingley, his sisters, and Mr. Darcy in the breakfast room. Elizabeth was busy attempting to steer her mother from embarrassing the Bennet family with her foolish comments when the subject of poetry having the ability to strengthen a relationship arose.

Elizabeth realizes that a strong relationship can only be strengthened, not diminished. Any means is capable of strengthening what is already strong. A weak relationship, on the other hand, can be easily damaged by various attempts to nourish it; especially if it is done in desperation.

"My ideas flow so rapidly that I have not time to express them-by which means my letters convey no ideas to my correspondents," Mr. Bingley said.

"Your humility, Mr. Bingley," said Elizabeth, "must disarm reproof."

"Nothing is more deceitful," said Mr. Darcy, "than the appearance of humility. It is often only carelessness of opinion, and sometimes an indirect boast."

"And which of the two do you call my little recent piece of modesty?" Bingley asked.

"The indirect boast," Mr. Darcy replied, "for you are really proud of your defects in writing, for you perceive them as proceeding from a rapidity of thought and carelessness of execution."

Take my yoke upon you, and learn from me,
for I am gentle and lowly in heart,
and you will find rest for your souls.
Matthew 11:29

❦

The second evening that Elizabeth had the opportunity of sitting with the party in Mr. Bingley's drawing room, the idea of being a good letter writer was discussed. Mr. Bingley stated that he often wrote so rapidly that he made mistakes, even left out words.

True humility can only be learned well by yoking with Jesus, the humble God of our salvation. Although Mr. Bingley's words appeared humble, he was truly bragging on his quick thinking. Jesus, the most-skilled Artisan in every area, is lowly enough to partner with us and teach us genuine humility.

DAY TWENTY-EIGHT

※

After playing some Italian songs, Miss Bingley varied the charm by a lively Scotch air; and soon afterwards Mr. Darcy, drawing near Elizabeth, said to her,--

"Do not you feel a great inclination, Miss Bennet, to seize such an opportunity of dancing a reel?"

She smiled, but made no answer. He repeated the question, with some surprise at her silence.

"Oh!" said she, "I heard you before, but I could not immediately determine what to say in reply. You wanted me, I know, to say 'Yes,' that you might have the pleasure of despising my taste; but I always delight in overthrowing those kind of schemes, and cheating a person of their premeditated contempt. I have, therefore, made up my mind to tell you, that I do not want to dance a reel at all--and now despise me if you dare."

"Indeed I do not dare."

Elizabeth, having rather expected to affront him, was amazed at his gallantry; but there was a mixture of sweetness and archness in her manner which made it difficult for her to affront anybody; and Darcy had never been so bewitched by any woman as he was by her. He really believed, that were it not for the inferiority of her connections, he should be in some danger.

Love is patient and kind...
1 Corinthians 13:4

☙❧

It is said that if you marry someone, you marry their family. Mr. Darcy, although enamored by Elizabeth's manners, shrunk from the thought of being linked to her because of her family connections. Mrs. Bennet had exposed herself as foolish, Catherine and Lydia had no real propriety, and even Elizabeth's more distant relatives were beneath Mr. Darcy's gentlemanly manner. His willingness to patiently admire Elizabeth should have given him the strength to endure her family's folly.

"I have faults enough, but they are not, I hope, of understanding. My temper I dare not vouch for. It is, I believe, too little yielding-certainly too little for the convenience of the world. I cannot forget the follies and vices of others so soon as I ought, nor their offenses against myself. My temper would perhaps be called resentful. My good opinion once lost is lost forever."

"That is a failing indeed!" cried Elizabeth. "Implacable resentment is a shade in a character. But you have chosen your fault well. I really cannot laugh at it. You are safe from me."

"There is in every disposition a tendency to some particular evil, a natural defect, which not even the best education can overcome."

"And *your* defect is a propensity to hate everybody."

"And yours," he replied with a smile, "is to willfully misunderstand them."

. . . bearing with one another and, if one has a complaint against another, forgiving each other; as the Lord has forgiven you, so you also must forgive.
Colossians 3:13

❧❧

In declaring his weakness, Mr. Darcy almost seems to be boasting. Elizabeth described him as implacable: not capable of being appeased. Although the rather serious conversation ends with a playful accusation by both, Mr. Darcy, by being proud about this weakness, is acting contrary to the Scriptural admonition of being tolerant and forgiving, just as Jesus our Savior is.

DAY THIRTY

❧❦

The master of the house heard with real sorrow that they were to go so soon, and repeatedly tried to persuade Miss Bennet that it would not be safe for her--that she was not enough recovered; but Jane was firm where she felt herself to be right.

To Mr. Darcy it was welcome intelligence-Elizabeth had been at Netherfield long enough. She attracted him more than he liked-and Miss Bingley was uncivil to *her*, and more teasing than usual to himself.

On Sunday, after morning service, the separation, so agreeable to almost all, took place. . . Elizabeth took leave of the whole party with the liveliest spirits.

Their father, though very laconic in his expressions of pleasure, was really glad to see them; he had felt their importance in the family circle. The evening conversation had lost much of its animation, and almost all its sense, by the absence of Jane and Elizabeth.

Whoever gives an honest answer kisses the lips.
Proverbs 24:26

❧

The departure of Jane and Elizabeth from Netherfield was accompanied by so many emotions. Both Mr. Darcy and Elizabeth were pleased to part from one another, for differing reasons.

But Mr. Bennet, although not very expressive, admired and appreciated the wisdom and balanced personalities of Jane and Elizabeth. Their absence from the family conversations in the evenings accentuated the foolishness of his younger daughters, and reinforced the pleasantness of conversing with his older, wiser children. Being wise, being able to speak wisely, is a true adornment for any woman.

"He must be an oddity, I think," said she. "I cannot make him out.--There is something very pompous in his style.--And what can he mean by apologizing for being next in the entail?-- We cannot suppose he would help it if he could.--Could he be a sensible man, sir?"

"No, my dear, I think not. I have great hopes of finding him quite the reverse. There is a mixture of servility and self-importance in his letter, which promises well. I am impatient to see him."

Incline your ear, and hear the words of the wise,
and apply your heart to my knowledge,
for it will be pleasant if you keep them within you,
if all of them are ready on your lips.
Proverbs 22:17-18

~~~

Mr. Bennet had inherited his house and property, Longbourn, through entail (the property must be handed down to a male heir). It was his hope to marry and have a son and keep the property in his family. But after five daughters, he accepted that Longbourn would pass to a more distant, male heir: namely a Mr. Collins.

Mr. Collins wrote and offered to visit and re-establish peace between himself and the Bennets. His letter stated his intention of apologizing for being the next heir.

Mr. Collins was a mixture of knowledge, foolishness, and false humility. His attempt to introduce peace seemed insincere; he only came across as condescending and fake. He had knowledge but lacked the wisdom to speak with humility.

※

"You judge very properly," said Mr. Bennet, "and it is happy for you that you possess the talent of flattering with delicacy. May I ask whether these pleasing attentions proceed from the impulse of the moment, or are the result of previous study?"

"They arise chiefly from what is passing at the time, and though I sometimes amuse myself with suggesting and arranging such little elegant compliments as maybe adapted to ordinary occasions, I always wish to give them as unstudied an air as possible."

Mr. Bennet's expectations were fully answered. His cousin was as absurd as he had hoped, and he listened to him with the keenest enjoyment, maintaining at the same time the most resolute composure of countenance, and, except in an occasional glance at Elizabeth, requiring no partner in his pleasure.

*It is better for a man to hear the rebuke of the wise
than to hear the song of fools.*
Ecclesiastes 7:5

☙❧

Mr. Collins' foolishness was obvious to those of the Bennet family who were wise, notably Mr. Bennet and Elizabeth. Although finding some pleasure in internally laughing at Mr. Collins' folly, and in sharing that joy with Elizabeth, Mr. Bennet soon grew tired of him. Foolishness is exhausting to the wise. May our weaknesses always be as obvious to us as they are to others.

Mr. Collins was not a sensible man, and the deficiency of nature had been but little assisted by education or society; the greatest part of his life having been spent under the guidance of an illiterate and miserly father; and though he belonged to one of the universities, he had merely kept the necessary terms, without forming at it any useful acquaintance. The subjection in which his father had brought him up had given him originally great humility of manner; but it was now a good deal counteracted by the self-conceit of a weak head, living in retirement, and the consequential feelings of early and unexpected prosperity. . .

Having now a good house and a very sufficient income, he intended to marry; and in seeking a reconciliation with the Longbourn family he had a wife in view, as he meant to choose one of the daughters, if he found them as handsome and amiable as they were represented by common report. This was his plan of amends--of atonement--for inheriting their father's estate; and he thought it an excellent one, full of eligibility and excessively generous and disinterested on his own part.

Create in me a clean heart, O God,
and renew a right spirit within me.
Psalm 51:10

❧※❦

Mr. Collins' foibles could only be mended by mirroring the genuine humility of King David. Changing his ways slowly would take too long; Mr. Collins needed a complete overhaul of heart and spirit. Such a spring cleaning of the soul would influence his personality for the good and make his demeanor more genuinely pleasing to those around him. True humility begins with honestly seeing ourselves in the light of a perfect God.

DAY THIRTY-FOUR

❧❧

AUTHOR'S SUMMARY OF EVENTS FROM PRIDE AND PREJUDICE:

When the four sisters (except Mary) and Mr. Collins walked to Meryton, Mr. Denny introduced them to a handsome, new officer, named Mr. Wickham. Just then Mr. Bingley and Mr. Darcy rode up the street and stopped to greet the group. The shocked and angry look that passed between Mr. Darcy and Mr. Wickham surprised Elizabeth. Both changed color, one looked white; the other red. Mr. Wickham, after a few moments, touched his hat-a salutation which Mr. Darcy merely deigned to return. What could be the meaning of it, Elizabeth wondered.

In another minute, Mr. Bingley, but without seeming to notice what passed, took leave and rode on with his friend.

The party of sisters and the two officers then stopped in to call on their mother's sister, Mrs. Philips, where they all received an invitation for the following evening for a light supper and cards. Elizabeth hoped to learn from Mr. Wickham, then, about the exchange between Mr. Darcy and himself.

Let all bitterness and wrath and anger and clamor and slander be put away from you, along with all malice.
Ephesians 4:31

What Elizabeth had witnessed but did not understand, was related to an old offense between the two men, which had turned to bitterness. She was eager to learn the meaning behind the obviously tense meeting between them. The Bible advises to lay aside the resentment from being wounded by others. Bitterness is an acid that eats away at its container.

"Oh! no--it is not for me to be driven away by Mr. Darcy. If he wishes to avoid seeing me, he must go. We are not on friendly terms, and it always gives me pain to meet him, but I have no reason for avoiding him but what I might proclaim before all the world, a sense of very great ill-usage, and most painful regrets at his being what he is. His father, Miss Bennet, the late Mr. Darcy, was one of the best men that ever breathed, and the truest friend I ever had; and I can never be in company with this Mr. Darcy without being grieved to the soul by a thousand tender recollections. His behavior to myself has been scandalous; but I verily believe I could forgive him anything and everything, rather than his disappointing the hopes and disgracing the memory of his father."

Elizabeth found the interest of the subject increase, and listened with all her heart; but the delicacy of it prevented farther inquiry.

*So put away all malice and all deceit and
hypocrisy and envy and all slander.*
I Peter 2:1

At first Elizabeth was surprised at Wickham's willingness to speak so freely but was herself quickly caught up in the anger that Wickham felt. Her initial dislike for Mr. Darcy was soon turning to disgust.

Elizabeth did not realize that she was being manipulated by Mr. Wickham's version of his tale of woe. There are always two sides to a story; Elizabeth was falling for the one side without question, based solely on a pre-determined dislike for Mr. Darcy. Wickham's story aligned with the picture of Mr. Darcy that she had chosen to accept. Lying, for the purpose of demeaning others and promoting oneself, is the lowest form of deceit, and Elizabeth was unknowingly becoming a slave to that lie.

DAY THIRTY-SIX

❧

Elizabeth related to Jane the next day, what had passed between Mr. Wickham and herself. Jane listened with astonishment and concern-she knew not how to believe that Mr. Darcy could be so unworthy of his friend, Mr. Bingley or deserve his regard; and yet it was not in her nature to question the veracity of a young man of such amiable appearance as Wickham. The possibility of his having really endured such unkindness, was enough to interest all her tender feelings. . .

"They have both," said she, "been deceived, I dare say, in some way or other, of which we can form no idea. . . It is, in short, impossible for us to conjecture the causes or circumstances which may have alienated them, without actual blame on either side."

". . . Do clear *them* too, or we shall be obliged to think ill of somebody?"

"Laugh as much as you choose, but you will not laugh me out of my opinion. My dearest Lizzy, do but consider in what a disgraceful light it places Mr. Darcy, to be treating his father's favorite in such a manner-one, whom his father had promised to provide for. It is impossible. No man of common humanity, no man who had any value for his character, could be capable of it. Can his most intimate friends be so excessively deceived in him?"

*Do not judge by appearances, but judge
with right judgment.*
John 7:24

❧

Jane's more simple nature caused her to seek for some reasonable explanation for Mr. Darcy's treatment of Wickham. Jane liked to think ill of no one, and yet her sympathetic nature felt the wounds suffered by Mr. Wickham. While Elizabeth had already judged the situation and condemned Mr. Darcy, Jane kept an open mind, following Christ's admonition; she sought a more balanced answer to the puzzling account of the two men's relationship.

DAY THIRTY-SEVEN

AUTHOR'S SUMMARY OF EVENTS FROM PRIDE AND PREJUDICE:

On Tuesday of that week, Mr. Bingley and his sisters came to give the invitation for the long-awaited ball at Netherfield, his home. The prospect of the ball was extremely agreeable to every female of the Bennet family. Mrs. Bennet chose to consider it a compliment to Jane. Elizabeth thought with great pleasure of dancing a great deal with Mr. Wickham, and the younger sisters dreamed of dances with officers. But Mr. Collins soon put a damper on Elizabeth's joy by declaring that he wished to claim the first two dances with her. She was mortified, and it now first struck her, that she was selected from among her sisters to be his wife and the mistress of his home, Hunsford Parsonage. This idea soon became a conviction as she observed his frequent attempts to compliment her wit and vivacity. Her mother then began to hint that she would approve of such a marriage. Elizabeth chose to not take her mother's hint and to not quarrel about it until Mr. Collins decided to actually make her an offer of marriage.

*"Therefore do not be anxious about tomorrow,
for tomorrow will be anxious for itself.
Sufficient for the day is its own trouble.*
Matthew 6:34

☙❧

Elizabeth had plans of spending time with Wickham at Bingley's ball, and watching Mr. Darcy squirm with embarrassment. But when Mr. Collins claimed the first two dances, Elizabeth bitterly realized that she was his object. She had been selected by Mr. Collins to grace his side and home. Although Elizabeth would have dearly loved to criticize her mother's approval of this idea, she decided it was useless to quarrel before the deed was officially done. Elizabeth had chosen to tuck the troubles of another day into the confinement of that future day.

DAY THIRTY-EIGHT

❧

Till Elizabeth entered the drawing-room at Netherfield, and looked in vain for Mr. Wickham among the cluster of red coats there assembled, a doubt of his being present had never occurred to her. The certainty of meeting him had not been checked by any of those recollections that might not unreasonably have alarmed her. She had dressed with more than usual care, and prepared in the highest spirits for the conquest of all that remained unsubdued of his heart, trusting that it was not more than might be won in the course of the evening. But in an instant arose the dreadful suspicion of his being purposely omitted for Mr. Darcy's pleasure in the Bingleys' invitation to the officers; and though this was not exactly the case, the absolute fact of his absence was pronounced by his friend Denny, to whom Lydia eagerly applied, and who told them that Wickham had been obliged to go to town on business the day before, and was not yet returned; adding, with a significant smile,

"I do not imagine his business would have called him away just now, if he had not wanted to avoid a certain gentleman here."

. . . But Elizabeth was not formed for ill-humor; and though every prospect of her own was destroyed for the evening, it could not dwell long on her spirits; and having told all her griefs to Charlotte Lucas, whom she had not seen for a week, she was soon able to make a voluntary transition to the oddities of her cousin, and to point him out to her particular notice.

A glad heart makes a cheerful face,
but by sorrow of heart the spirit is crushed.
Proverbs 15:13

❦

Although outward circumstances had destroyed Elizabeth's hopes for enjoying her evening, her inward, cheerful heart was able to help her transition from having a bad attitude to her typical, fun-loving self. Possessing a merry heart, even cultivating one, can carry a person through life's little disappointments. Outward influences cannot be controlled, but inward responses can.

DAY THIRTY-NINE

֎

The first two dances, however, brought a return of distress; they were dances of mortification. Mr. Collins, awkward and solemn, apologizing instead of attending, and often moving wrong without being aware of it, gave her all the shame and misery which a disagreeable partner for a couple of dances can give. The moment of her release from him was ecstasy.

She danced next with an officer, and had the refreshment of talking of Wickham, and of hearing that he was universally liked. When those dances were over, she returned to Charlotte Lucas, and was in conversation with her, when she found herself suddenly addressed by Mr. Darcy who took her so much by surprise in his application for her hand, that, without knowing what she did, she accepted him. He walked away again immediately, and she was left to fret over her own want of presence of mind; Charlotte tried to console her:

"I dare say you will find him very agreeable."

"Heaven forbid! *That* would be the greatest misfortune of all! To find a man agreeable whom one is determined to hate! Do not wish me such an evil."

When the dancing recommenced, however, and Darcy approached to claim her hand, Charlotte could not help cautioning her in a whisper, not to be a simpleton, and allow her fancy for Wickham to make her appear unpleasant in the eyes of a man ten times his consequence.

Hatred stirs up strife, but love covers all offenses.
Proverbs 10:12

❧

Elizabeth's determination to dislike Mr. Darcy and to think evil of him due to Mr. Wickham's accusations, was detrimental to their potential relationship. Although Charlotte cautions her to give him a chance, to consider what a compliment that he was paying her, Elizabeth was bent on her prejudice against Darcy. She permitted her hatred to create even more issues and complications when she could have relied on love and mercy to give Mr. Darcy a chance.

❧

"I remember hearing you once say, Mr. Darcy, that you hardly ever forgave, that your resentment once created was unappeasable. You are very cautious, I suppose, as to its *being created* ."

"I am," said he, with a firm voice.

"And never allow yourself to be blinded by prejudice?"

"I hope not."

"It is particularly incumbent on those who never change their opinion, to be secure of judging properly at first."

"May I ask to what these questions tend?"

"Merely to the illustration of your character," said she, endeavoring to shake off her gravity. "I am trying to make it out."

"And what is your success?"

She shook her head. "I do not get on at all. I hear such different accounts of you as puzzle me exceedingly."

*You shall not take vengeance or bear a grudge
against the sons of your own people, but you shall
love your neighbor as yourself: I am the Lord.*
Leviticus 19:18

❧

During Elizabeth's half-hour dance with Mr. Darcy, she brought up the chance meeting of Darcy and Wickham a few days earlier. The effect of such a topic being raised was immediate. A deep shade of hauteur over spread his features, but he said not a word.

Elizabeth found herself less than satisfied with her understanding of Mr. Darcy's character after the dance was finished. Mr. Darcy had many reasons to hang on to his resentment against Wickham, but God would have taken Mr. Darcy to task for bearing a grudge… justifying his anger. God, for Christ's sake, forgave us, creating the understanding heart that is needed to forgive others.

DAY FORTY-ONE

❧❧

Mr. Bingley does not know the whole of his history, and is quite ignorant of the circumstances which have principally offended Mr. Darcy; but he will vouch for the good conduct, the probity, and honor of his friend, and is perfectly convinced that Mr. Wickham has deserved much less attention from Mr. Darcy than he has received; and I am sorry to say by his account as well as his sister's, Mr. Wickham is by no means a respectable young man. I am afraid he has been very imprudent, and has deserved to lose Mr. Darcy's regard."

"Mr. Bingley does not know Mr. Wickham himself?"

"No; he never saw him till the other morning at Meryton."

"This account then is what he has received from Mr. Darcy. I am satisfied. But what does he say of the living?"

"He does not exactly recollect the circumstances, though he has heard them from Mr. Darcy more than once, but he believes that it was left to him *conditionally* only."

"I have not a doubt of Mr. Bingley's sincerity," said Elizabeth warmly; "but you must excuse my not being convinced by assurances only. Mr. Bingley's defense of his friend was a very able one, I dare say; but since he is unacquainted with several parts of the story, and has learnt the rest from that friend himself, I shall venture to still think of both gentlemen as I did before."

*A man of many companions may come to ruin,
but there is a friend who sticks closer than
a brother.*
Proverbs 18:24

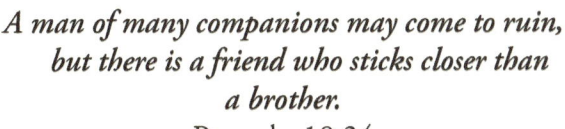

Mr. Bingley, though of a simpler personality than Mr. Darcy, is a loyal friend. He trusts Darcy's account of the situation of Wickham, proving that he trusts Darcy to be truthful. Wickham has been imprudent and undeserving of the pastorate. Sadly, Elizabeth chooses to assume that Mr. Bingley has been duped by Darcy. She continues in her pre-determined dislike of Mr. Darcy and her high regard of Wickham. She forgets that close friends are close because of their open, honest, transparent relationships.

DAY FORTY-TWO

&&

"You are not going to introduce yourself to Mr. Darcy!"

"Indeed I am. I shall entreat his pardon for not having done it earlier. I believe him to be Lady Catherine's *nephew*. It will be in my power to assure him that her ladyship was quite well yesterday se'nnight."

Elizabeth tried hard to dissuade him from such a scheme, assuring him that Mr. Darcy would consider his addressing him without introduction as an impertinent freedom, rather than a compliment to his aunt; that it was not in the least necessary there should be any notice on either side; and that if it were, it must belong to Mr. Darcy, the superior in consequence, to begin the acquaintance. Mr. Collins listened to her with the determined air of following his own inclination, and, when she ceased speaking, replied thus: "My dear Miss Elizabeth, I have the highest opinion in the world in your excellent judgement in all matters within the scope of your understanding; but permit me to say, that there must be a wide difference between the established forms of ceremony amongst the laity, and those which regulate the clergy; for, give me leave to observe that I consider the clerical office as equal in point of dignity with the highest rank in the kingdom--provided that a proper humility of behavior is at the same time maintained. . ."

*When you are invited by someone to a wedding
feast, do not sit down in a place of honor...
[but] sit in the lowest place...
For everyone who exalts himself will be humbled,
and he who humbles himself will be exalted.*
Luke 14:8-11

Although Elizabeth attempted to discourage Mr. Collins from exposing himself as a fool, he arrogantly moved forward with his plan to introduce himself, improperly, to Mr. Darcy. His pride in his position as a pastor strengthened Mr. Collins to promote himself. Elizabeth witnessed and understood how severely Darcy judged Mr. Collins for his impropriety, but Mr. Collins himself was too smug to even recognize the insult. May we always be wise enough and humble enough to acknowledge how foolish we truly are.

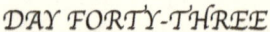

"What is Mr. Darcy to me, pray, that I should be afraid of him? I am sure we owe him no such particular civility as to be obliged to say nothing he may not like to hear."

"For heaven's sake, madam, speak lower. What advantage can it be for you to offend Mr. Darcy? You will never recommend yourself to his friend by so doing!"

Nothing that she could say, however, had any influence. Her mother would talk of her views in the same intelligible tone. Elizabeth blushed and blushed again with shame and vexation. She could not help frequently glancing her eye at Mr. Darcy, though every glance convinced her of what she dreaded; for though he was not always looking at her mother, she was convinced that his attention was invariably fixed by her. The expression of his face changed gradually from indignant contempt to a composed and steady gravity.

The woman Folly is loud; she is seductive and knows nothing.
Proverbs 9:13

※

At the same ball, Elizabeth was once again embarrassed by her family, when she heard her mother discussing Jane and Bingley's future marriage, in a loud whisper, within earshot of Mr. Darcy.

Mrs. Bennet is the epitome of the foolish woman. She believes that she is smart; smarter than her wise daughter but is unaware of how truly foolish she is by speaking so presumptuously about Jane and Bingley, within the vicinity of Mr. Darcy. She does not realize that she is putting her daughter's future in jeopardy. Sometimes a foolish mother can learn from a wise, discerning daughter, like Elizabeth.

To Elizabeth it appeared that, had her family made an agreement to expose themselves as much as they could during the evening, it would have been impossible for them to play their parts with more spirit or finer success; and happy did she think it for Bingley and her sister that some of the exhibition had escaped his notice, and that his feelings were not of a sort to be much distressed by the folly which he must have witnessed. That his two sisters and Mr. Darcy, however, should have such an opportunity of ridiculing her relations, was bad enough, and she could not determine whether the silent contempt of the gentleman, or the insolent smiles of the ladies, were more intolerable.

The rest of the evening brought her little amusement. She was teased by Mr. Collins, who continued most perseveringly by her side, and though he could not prevail on her to dance with him again, put it out of her power to dance with others.

*A prudent man conceals knowledge,
but the heart of fools proclaims folly.*
Proverbs 12:23

☙❧

Elizabeth barely had a chance to recover from the shame of her mother, when Mary decided to "grace" the party by playing the piano and singing two songs. By significant looks, Elizabeth tried to stop her, but in vain. Mary's voice was weak, and her manner affected. At last Mr. Bennet took a hint from Elizabeth and stopped Mary before she could start into a third song.

Within the walls of her own house, the foolishness of Elizabeth's family was not obvious, but at the Netherfield ball, their follies were exposed to ridicule. Her mother's blatant bragging about Jane's future, Mary's pompous attitude about sharing her musical "talents" and the open flirtation of Lydia and Catherine with every available officer made the evening a torture for Elizabeth. Foolishness in the heart always finds a way out of the mouth, bringing scorn from the wise who hear it.

DAY FORTY-FIVE

ಎಲ್

The next day opened a new scene at Longbourn. Mr. Collins made his declaration in form. Having resolved to do it without loss of time, as his leave of absence extended only to the following Saturday, and having no feelings of diffidence to make it distressing to himself even at the moment, he set about it in a very orderly manner, with all the observances, which he supposed a regular part of the business. On finding Mrs. Bennet, Elizabeth, and one of the younger girls together, soon after breakfast, he addressed the mother in these words: "May I hope, madam, for your interest with your fair daughter Elizabeth, when I solicit for the honor of a private audience with her in the course of this morning?"

Before Elizabeth had time for anything but a blush of surprise, Mrs. Bennet answered instantly, "Oh dear!--yes--certainly. I am sure Lizzy will be very happy--I am sure she can have no objection. Come, Kitty, I want you upstairs." And, gathering her work together, she was hastening away, when Elizabeth called out:

"Dear madam, do not go. I beg you will not go. Mr. Collins must excuse me. He can have nothing to say to me that anybody need not hear. I am going away myself."

"No, no, nonsense, Lizzy. I desire you to stay where you are." And upon Elizabeth's seeming really, with vexed and embarrassed looks, about to escape, she added: "Lizzy, I insist upon your staying and hearing Mr. Collins."

. . . The idea of Mr. Collins, with all his solemn composure, being run away with by his feelings, made Elizabeth so near laughing, that she could not use the short pause he allowed in any attempt to stop him further. . .

A glad heart makes a cheerful face . . . The heart of him who has understanding seeks knowledge, but the mouths of fools feed on folly.
Proverbs 15:13a, 14

❧⊷❧

Elizabeth knew that she must obey her mother and listen to Mr. Collins' proposal, but she was greatly distressed by the idea. Her pleasant nature, though, latched on to one amusing phrase in the long and foolish speech that was an affront to her intelligence. Elizabeth's ability to endure such a social torture was strengthened by her finding the "funny" in the foolishness of this proud man. Even in this vexing situation, Elizabeth found a bit of joy in observing the mouth of the foolish pouring out folly.

DAY FORTY-SIX

༄༅

"My reasons for marrying are, first, that I think it a right thing for every clergyman in easy circumstances (like myself) to set the example of matrimony in his parish; secondly, that I am convinced that it will add very greatly to my happiness; and thirdly--which perhaps I ought to have mentioned earlier, that it is the particular advice and recommendation of the very noble lady whom I have the honor of calling patroness. . . 'Mr. Collins, you must marry. A clergyman like you must marry. Choose properly, choose a gentlewoman for *my* sake. . . Thus much for my general intention in favor of matrimony; it remains to be told why my views were directed towards Longbourn instead of my own neighborhood, where I can assure you there are many amiable young women. But the fact is, that being, as I am, to inherit this estate after the death of your honored father (who, however, may live many years longer), I could not satisfy myself without resolving to choose a wife from among his daughters, that the loss to them might be as little as possible, when the melancholy event takes place--which, however, as I have already said, may not be for several years. This has been my motive, my fair cousin, and I flatter myself it will not sink me in your esteem. And now nothing remains for me but to assure you in the most animated language of the violence of my affection."

*Let each of you look not only to his own interests,
but also to the interests of others.*
Philippians 2:4

෧෧෨

Mr. Collins' pride and selfishness blinded him to his true character. His desire to marry Elizabeth had nothing to do with her happiness, only his own. May we be honest enough to see our own faults, and wise enough to love someone else selflessly for who they truly are. To accept anything less in ourselves and our future partner is to accept a life of true misery.

DAY FORTY-SEVEN

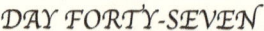

"You are too hasty, sir," she cried. "You forget that I have made no answer. Let me do it without further loss of time. Accept my thanks for the compliment you are paying me. I am very sensible of the honor of your proposals, but it is impossible for me to do otherwise than to decline them."

"I am not now to learn," replied Mr. Collins, with a formal wave of the hand, "that it is usual with young ladies to reject the addresses of the man whom they secretly mean to accept, when he first applies for their favor; and that sometimes the refusal is repeated a second, or even a third time. I am therefore by no means discouraged by what you have just said, and shall hope to lead you to the altar ere long."

"Upon my word, sir," cried Elizabeth, "your hope is a rather extraordinary one after my declaration. . . You must give me leave to judge for myself, and pay me the compliment of believing what I say."

Therefore, having put away falsehood, let each one of you speak the truth with his neighbor, for we are members one of another.
Ephesians 4:25

Elizabeth was not used to being disbelieved; her reputation for being honest was well known. Strangely, Mr. Collins' pride, which continuously lied to his mind, could not comprehend a young woman, who would not jump at the idea of becoming his wife. It is possible that one person's pride can influence his thinking, causing him to assume that another is not being truthful. May we never believe the lies that our pride can whisper to us.

DAY FORTY-EIGHT

༄༅

Mr. Collins was not left long to the silent contemplation of his successful love; for Mrs. Bennet, having dawdled about in the vestibule to watch for the end of the conference, no sooner saw Elizabeth open the door and with quick step pass her towards the staircase, than she entered the breakfast-room, and congratulated both him and herself in warm terms on the happy prospect or their nearer connection. Mr. Collins received and returned these felicitations with equal pleasure, and then proceeded to relate the particulars of their interview, with the result of which he trusted he had every reason to be satisfied, since the refusal which his cousin had steadfastly given him would naturally flow from her bashful modesty and the genuine delicacy of her character.

This information, however, startled Mrs. Bennet; she would have been glad to be equally satisfied that her daughter had meant to encourage him by protesting against his proposals, but she dared not believe it, and could not help saying so.

"But, depend upon it, Mr. Collins," she added, "that Lizzy shall be brought to reason. I will speak to her about it directly. She is a very headstrong, foolish girl, and does not know her own interest but I will make her know it."

"Pardon me for interrupting you, madam," cried Mr. Collins; "but if she is really headstrong and foolish, I know not whether she would altogether be a very desirable wife to a man in my situation, who naturally looks for happiness in the marriage state. If therefore she actually persists in rejecting my suit, perhaps it were better not to force her into accepting me, because if liable to such defects of temper, she could not contribute much to my felicity."

However, let each one of you love his wife as himself, and let the wife see that she respects her husband.
Ephesians 5:33

☙❧

Mr. Collins' pride had convinced him that Elizabeth's rejection was merely a joke, but Mrs. Bennet's assurance that Elizabeth was sincere, made him conclude that Elizabeth must be too foolish to make him truly happy. Certainly Mr. Collins did not love Elizabeth as much as he loved himself. It was obvious that Elizabeth did not respect him. Elizabeth was wise enough to turn down this self-centered man rather than enter a marriage that could only lead to misery.

When Mrs. Bennet implored her husband to make Elizabeth marry Mr. Collins, Mr. Bennet took Elizabeth's side which sent Mrs. Bennet into a foul mood for the rest of the day, while Mr. Collins only seemed to suffer from wounded pride. His regard for Elizabeth was quite imaginary.

DAY FORTY-NINE

The discussion of Mr. Collins's offer was now nearly at an end, and Elizabeth had only to suffer from the uncomfortable feelings necessarily attending it, and occasionally from some peevish allusions of her mother. As for the gentleman himself, his feelings were chiefly expressed, not by embarrassment or dejection, or by trying to avoid her, but by stiffness of manner and resentful silence. He scarcely ever spoke to her, and the assiduous attentions which he had been so sensible of himself were transferred for the rest of the day to Miss Lucas, whose civility in listening to him was a seasonable relief to them all, and especially to her friend.

The morrow produced no abatement of Mrs. Bennet's ill-humor or ill health. Mr. Collins was also in the same state of angry pride. Elizabeth had hoped that his resentment might shorten his visit, but his plan did not appear in the least affected by it. He was always to have gone on Saturday, and to Saturday he meant to stay.

[Love] does not insist on its own way;
it is not irritable or resentful. . .
I Corinthians 13:5

Mr. Collins is displaying his self-centeredness and lack of genuine love for Elizabeth by being angry and resentful. (Her mother, conversely, shows her motive for having Elizabeth marry such a foolish man, to be purely pecuniary and self-preserving.) The chapter on love declares that true love does not seek its own agenda, is not irritable or resentful. According to these standards, Mr. Collins does not even know the definition of genuine, selfless love.

DAY FIFTY

☙❧

Soon after their return, a letter was delivered to Miss Bennet; it came from Netherfield. The envelope contained a sheet of elegant, little, hot-pressed paper, well covered with a lady's fair, flowing hand; and Elizabeth saw her sister's countenance change as she read it, and saw her dwelling intently on some particular passages. Jane recollected herself soon, and putting the letter away, tried to join with her usual cheerfulness in the general conversation; but Elizabeth felt an anxiety on the subject which drew off her attention even from Wickham; and no sooner had he and his companion taken leave, than a glance from Jane invited her to follow her upstairs. When they had gained their own room, Jane, taking out the letter, said: "This is from Caroline Bingley; what it contains has surprised me a good deal. The whole party have left Netherfield by this time, and are on their way to town--and without any intention of coming back again. You shall hear what she says."

. . .To these high-flown expressions Elizabeth listened with all the insensibility of distrust; and though the suddenness of their removal surprised her, she saw nothing in it really to lament; it was not to be supposed that their absence from Netherfield would prevent Mr. Bingley's being there; and as to the loss of their society, she was persuaded that Jane must cease to regard it, in the enjoyment of his.

*Hope deferred makes the heart sick,
but a desire fulfilled is a tree of life.*
Proverbs 13:12

Jane is extremely saddened when her hopes of being engaged to Mr. Bingley are delayed by his extended trip to London on business. The letter from Caroline Bingley causes Jane to be sorrowful but Elizabeth to be suspicious of Caroline's motives; having never trusted her smooth façade. Heart sickness is often the result of our hopes in a person or future event being delayed or postponed. Many verses in the Psalms encourage us to "hope in God," Who never disappoints.

※

"It is evident by this," added Jane, "that he comes back no more this winter."

"It is only evident that Miss Bingley does not mean that he *should*."

"Is it not clear enough? Does it not expressly declare that Caroline neither expects nor wishes me to be her sister; that she is perfectly convinced of her brother's indifference; and that if she suspects the nature of my feelings for him, she means (most kindly!) to put me on my guard? Can there be any other opinion on the subject?"

"Yes, there can; for mine is totally different. Will you hear it?"

"Most willingly."

"You shall have it in a few words. Miss Bingley sees that her brother is in love with you, and wants him to marry Miss Darcy. She follows him to town in hope of keeping him there, and tries to persuade you that he does not care about you."

"If we thought alike of Miss Bingley," replied Jane, "your representation of all this might make me quite easy. But I know the foundation is unjust. Caroline is incapable of willfully deceiving anyone; and all that I can hope in this case is that she is deceived herself."

Blessed is the man against whom the Lord counts no iniquity, and in whose spirit there is no deceit.
Psalm 32:2

❧⚜❧

Elizabeth suspects the truth about Caroline Bingley; that she is practicing deceit in her letter. She wants Jane to think that Bingley left Netherfield, purposefully to pursue Georgiana Darcy as a wife; leaving Jane with the idea that she means nothing to him. Elizabeth sees through the ploy and tries to comfort her sister with the hope of truth. May we always be sensible of the deceitful plans of the crafty people that enter our lives.

DAY FIFTY-TWO

❦

The Bennets were engaged to dine with the Lucases and again during the chief of the day was Miss Lucas so kind as to listen to Mr. Collins. Elizabeth took an opportunity of thanking her. "It keeps him in good humor," said she, "and I am more obliged to you than I can express." Charlotte assured her friend of her satisfaction in being useful, and that it amply repaid her for the little sacrifice of her time. This was very amiable, but Charlotte's kindness extended farther than Elizabeth had any conception of; its object was nothing else than to secure her from any return of Mr. Collins's addresses, by engaging them towards herself. Such was Miss Lucas's scheme; and appearances were so favorable, that when they parted at night, she would have felt almost secure of success if he had not been to leave Hertfordshire so very soon. But here she did injustice to the fire and independence of his character, for it led him to escape out of Longbourn House the next morning with admirable slyness, and hasten to Lucas Lodge to throw himself at her feet. . .

In as short a time as Mr. Collins's long speeches would allow, everything was settled between them to the satisfaction of both; and as they entered the house he earnestly entreated her to name the day that was to make him the happiest of men. . .

An excellent wife who can find?
She is far more precious than jewels.
Proverbs 31:10

❦

It appeared that Mr. Collins found a valuable virtuous woman in Charlotte Lucas (whether or not she found in him something valuable was up for question). Older than her friend Elizabeth by eight years, less romantic, and more practical, Charlotte saw in Mr. Collins what Elizabeth was not in a position to appreciate: an escape from spinsterhood and poverty. Charlotte latched onto Mr. Collins, accepting the consequences of being regularly mortified by her future husband's foolishness.

DAY FIFTY-THREE

~~~~~

Charlotte herself was tolerably composed. She had gained her point, and had time to consider of it. Her reflections were in general satisfactory. Mr. Collins, to be sure, was neither sensible nor agreeable; his society was irksome, and his attachment to her must be imaginary. But still he would be her husband. Without thinking highly either of men or matrimony, marriage had always been her object; it was the only provision for well-educated young women of small fortune, and however uncertain of giving happiness, must be their pleasantest preservative from want. This preservative she had now obtained; and at the age of twenty-seven, without having ever been handsome, she felt all the good luck of it. The least agreeable circumstance in the business was the surprise it must occasion to Elizabeth Bennet, whose friendship she valued beyond that of any other person. . .

"Engaged to Mr. Collins! My dear Charlotte--impossible!" . . .

"I see what you are feeling," replied Charlotte. "You must be surprised, very much surprised--so lately as Mr. Collins was wishing to marry you. But when you have had time to think it over, I hope you will be satisfied with what I have done. I am not romantic, you know; I never was. I ask only a comfortable home; and considering Mr. Collins's character, connection, and situation in life, I am convinced that my chance of happiness with him is as fair as most people can boast on entering the marriage state."

She does him good, and not harm,
all the days of her life.
Proverbs 31:12

Charlotte Lucas agrees to begin a marriage with Mr. Collins, hoping for happiness, while lacking the needed respect for him as a person. She confessed that he was neither intelligent nor easy to get along with, but her desire to escape poverty motivated her to agree to an engagement. Yet because Charlotte is strong, she is committed to doing him good for the rest of her life. Some may fault Charlotte Lucas for being more interested in a steady income than a happy marriage, but during that time period, a woman had few choices. Being able to respect your choice in a life's mate is vital to a happy marriage; may we not make Charlotte's mistake of hoping for happiness apart from admiration and respect for the one we choose to be with.

DAY FIFTY-FOUR

❧

Elizabeth was sitting with her mother and sisters, reflecting on what she had heard, and doubting whether she was authorized to mention it, when Sir William Lucas himself appeared, sent by his daughter, to announce her engagement to the family. With many compliments to them, and much self-gratulation on the prospect of a connection between the houses, he unfolded the matter--to an audience not merely wondering, but incredulous; for Mrs. Bennet, with more perseverance than politeness, protested he must be entirely mistaken; and Lydia, always unguarded and often uncivil, boisterously exclaimed:

"Good Lord! Sir William, how can you tell such a story? Do not you know that Mr. Collins wants to marry Lizzy?"

Nothing less than the complaisance of a courtier could have borne without anger such treatment; but Sir William's good breeding carried him through it all; and though he begged leave to be positive as to the truth of his information, he listened to all their impertinence with the most forbearing courtesy.

Elizabeth, feeling it incumbent on her to relieve him from so unpleasant a situation, now put herself forward to confirm his account, by mentioning her prior knowledge of it from Charlotte herself. . ."

*It is better to live in a corner of the housetop
than in a house shared with a quarrelsome wife.*
Proverbs 25:24

After Sir William left, Mrs. Bennet's feelings found a rapid vent: first she disbelieved the account, second that Mr. Collins had been tricked, third that the couple would never be happy, and fourth that she hoped the engagement would be broken. She finally settled on Elizabeth being the real cause of all the mischief. Mrs. Bennet dwelt on that the rest of the day. A week passed before she could see Elizabeth without scolding her for turning down Mr. Collins; months before she could speak to the Lucas' without being rude.

Mrs. Bennet, the epitome of narcissism, sees every setback as a direct attack on herself and her plans. She blames everyone around her for making her unhappy and has no filter to keep her from spewing her harshness on those around her. Elizabeth received the scolding, the Lucas' the rudeness, and Charlotte the resentment. Not being like Mrs. Bennet could be a basic life's goal.

DAY FIFTY-FIVE

AUTHOR'S SUMMARY OF EVENTS FROM PRIDE AND PREJUDICE:

Between Elizabeth and Charlotte there was a restraint which kept them mutually silent on the subject of Mr. Collins and the engagement. Elizabeth felt that no real confidence could ever subsist between them again.

In addition to the stress of the engagement of Charlotte and Mr. Collins, was Mr. Bingley's continued absence. The report prevailed around Meryton of his returning to Netherfield no more that winter; this incensed Mrs. Bennet, and put her in a foul disposition. Elizabeth did not bring up the painful subject much with Jane, but no such delicacy restrained her mother. An hour seldom passed in which she did not talk of Bingley and express impatience for his arrival. It needed all Jane's steady mildness to bear these attacks with tranquility.

Two weeks later, Mr. Collins returned for a visit to Longbourn with the purpose of courting Charlotte. The chief of every day was spent by him at Lucas Lodge, but whenever Charlotte came to visit the Bennet family, Mrs. Bennet concluded her to be anticipating the hour when she and Mr. Collins were to be in possession of the estate. She worried that she and her daughters would be turned out of the house as soon as Mr. Bennet died. It seemed that trouble had descended on Longbourn.

For the moment all discipline seems painful rather than pleasant, but later it yields the peaceful fruit of righteousness to those who have been trained by it.
Hebrews 12:11

❧❧

Life had taken a stressful turn for the Bennet family: Mr. Bingley did not return to his home in the neighborhood, causing Jane and her family to doubt whether he had truly showed signs of loving her. This caused Mrs. Bennet distress which she constantly expressed day in and day out, disturbing Jane. In addition, the engagement of Mr. Collins and Charlotte reminded Mrs. Bennet that one day they would inherit the Longbourn estate. The hardships and disappointments of life are never pleasant. Outside stress creeps into the home, affecting the conversation among family members. Trials are great teachers if we are wise learners of their lessons. Patience (a quality Mrs. Bennet lacked) is required to grasp the teachings of this life.

DAY FIFTY-SIX

❧❧

Miss Bingley's letter arrived, and put an end to doubt. The very first sentence conveyed the assurance of their being all settled in London for the winter, and concluded with her brother's regret at not having had time to pay his respects to his friends in Hertfordshire before he left the country.

Hope was over, entirely over; and when Jane could attend to the rest of the letter, she found little, except the professed affection of the writer, that could give her any comfort. . .

Elizabeth, to whom Jane very soon communicated the chief of all this, heard it in silent indignation. Her heart was divided between concern for her sister, and resentment against all others. To Caroline's assertion of her brother's being partial to Miss Darcy she paid no credit. That he was really fond of Jane, she doubted no more than she had ever done; and much as she had always been disposed to like him, she could not think without anger, hardly without contempt, on that easiness of temper, that want of proper resolution, which now made him the slave of his designing friends, and led him to sacrifice of his own happiness to the caprice of their inclinations.

The prudent sees danger and hides himself,
but the simple go on and suffer for it.
Proverbs 27:12

˚∂≈

Was Charles Bingley at fault because he walked into the trap set by his sisters and friend? Elizabeth believed that he was. Bingley's "easiness of temper" made him pliable to those who sought to control his future, as it related to Jane. It may be harsh to label Mr. Bingley as simple-minded. Perhaps he was just so easy-going that he allowed himself to be manipulated-to be kept away from Jane. May we always be prudent…able to discern the forces at work in our lives.

DAY FIFTY-SEVEN

༄༅

A day or two passed before Jane had courage to speak of her feelings to Elizabeth; but at last, on Mrs. Bennet's leaving them together, after a longer irritation than usual about Netherfield and its master, she could not help saying:

"Oh, that my dear mother had more command over herself! She can have no idea of the pain she gives me by her continual reflections on him. But I will not repine. It cannot last long. He will be forgot, and we shall all be as we were before."

Elizabeth looked at her sister with incredulous solicitude, but said nothing.

"You doubt me," cried Jane, slightly coloring; "indeed, you have no reason. He may live in my memory as the most amiable man of my acquaintance, but that is all. I have nothing either to hope or fear, and nothing to reproach him with. Thank God! I have not that pain. A little time, therefore--I shall certainly try to get the better."

With a stronger voice she soon added, "I have this comfort immediately, that it has not been more than an error of fancy on my side, and that it has done no harm to anyone but myself."

"My dear Jane!" exclaimed Elizabeth, "you are too good. Your sweetness and disinterestedness are really angelic; I do not know what to say to you. I feel as if I had never done you justice, or loved you as you deserve."

For you have need of endurance, so that when you have done the will of God you may receive what is promised.
Hebrews 10:36

※

Jane rises in the eyes of her sister Elizabeth for her simple patience in the light of her broken relationship with Bingley. Jane has given Mr. Bingley a place of honor in in her mind, as being friendly and respectful. She realizes that blaming him would extend the time of her healing. Jane's attempted position of being objective preserves her from further pain through bitterness. So, which is better? Quietly enduring life's disappointments? Or standing up and fighting for a solution? Maybe a bit of both: taking time to internally reflect first to allow healing, then through healing finding the needed strength to rise up and make some changes.

"My dear Lizzy, do not give way to such feelings as these. They will ruin your happiness. You do not make allowance enough for difference of situation and temper. Consider Mr. Collins's respectability, and Charlotte's steady, prudent character. Remember that she is one of a large family; that as to fortune, it is a most eligible match; and be ready to believe, for everybody's sake, that she may feel something like regard and esteem for our cousin."

"To oblige you, I would try to believe almost anything, but no one else could be benefited by such a belief as this; for were I persuaded that Charlotte had any regard for him, I should only think worse of her understanding than I now do of her heart. My dear Jane, Mr. Collins is a conceited, pompous, narrow-minded, silly man; you know he is, as well as I do; and you must feel, as well as I do, that the woman who married him cannot have a proper way of thinking. You shall not defend her, though it is Charlotte Lucas. You shall not, for the sake of one individual, change the meaning of principle and integrity, nor endeavor to persuade yourself or me, that selfishness is prudence, and insensibility of danger security for happiness."

*Better is a dry morsel with quiet
than a house full of feasting with strife.*
Proverbs 17:1

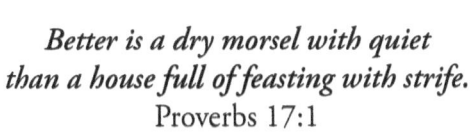

Elizabeth believes that her friend Charlotte is foolish to sacrifice freedom of thinking and behavior for an entire lifetime, to gain financial security through marriage. Charlotte believes that she is willing to pay the expensive price of continual strife to obtain a living. Quietly submitting to and continually enduring Mr. Collins' folly is a high price indeed! Proverbs encourages us to choose living peacefully in poverty, rather than to choose nightly feasting with the strife of living with a fool.

❧☙

"I am far from attributing any part of Mr. Bingley's conduct to design," said Elizabeth; "but without scheming to do wrong, or to make others unhappy, there may be error, and there may be misery. Thoughtlessness, want of attention to other people's feelings, and want of resolution, will do the business."

"And do you impute it to either of those?"

"Yes; to the last. But if I go on, I shall displease you by saying what I think of persons you esteem. Stop me whilst you can."

"You persist, then, in supposing his sisters influence him?"

"Yes, in conjunction with his friend."

"I cannot believe it. Why should they try to influence him? They can only wish his happiness; and if he is attached to me, no other woman can secure it."

"Your first position is false. They may wish many things besides his happiness; they may wish his increase of wealth and consequence; they may wish him to marry a girl who has all the importance of money, great connections, and pride."

*Many are the plans in the mind of a man,
but it is the purpose of the Lord that will stand.*
Proverbs 19:21

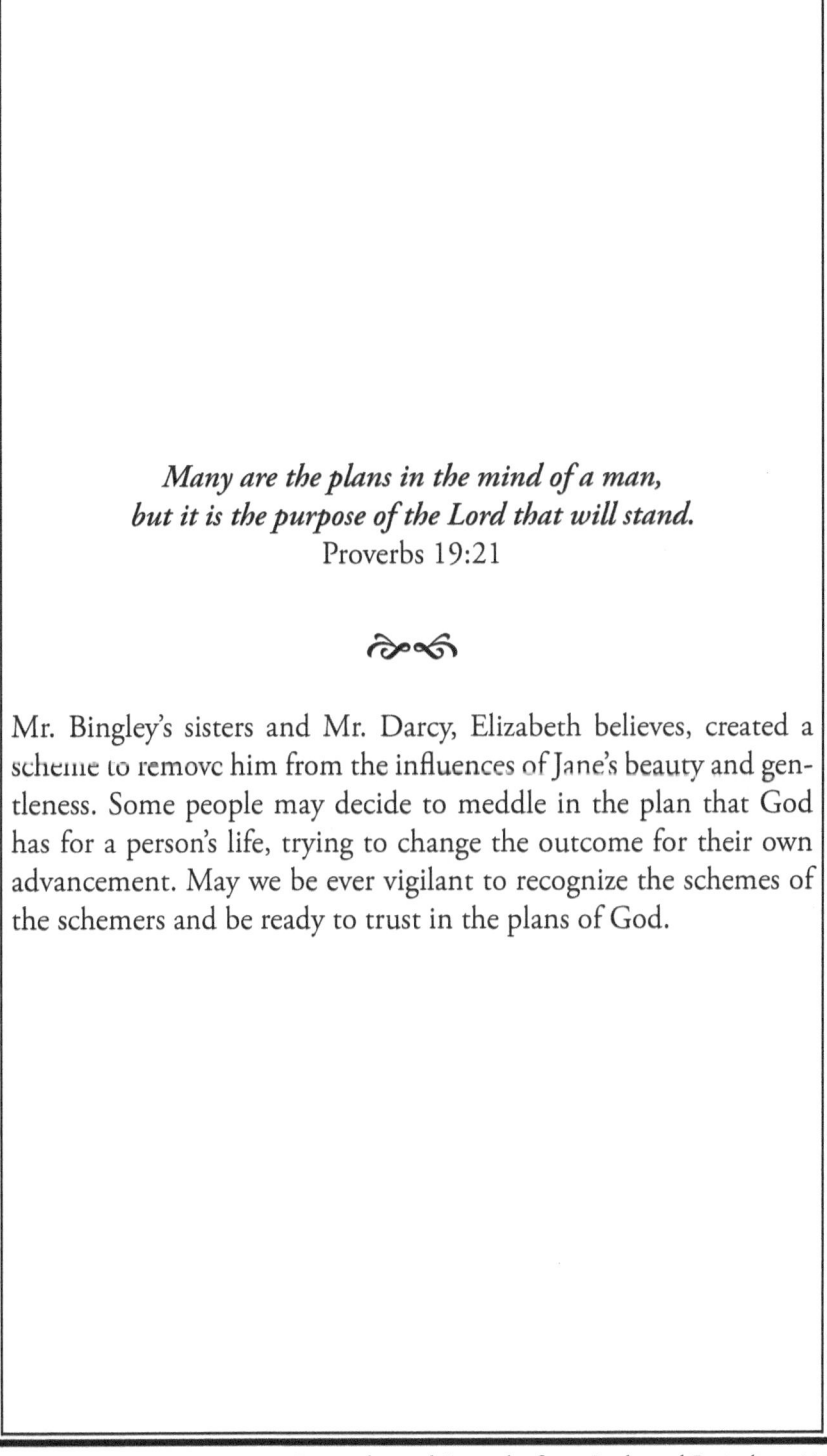

Mr. Bingley's sisters and Mr. Darcy, Elizabeth believes, created a scheme to remove him from the influences of Jane's beauty and gentleness. Some people may decide to meddle in the plan that God has for a person's life, trying to change the outcome for their own advancement. May we be ever vigilant to recognize the schemes of the schemers and be ready to trust in the plans of God.

DAY SIXTY

⧢

Mrs. Bennet still continued to wonder and repine at his returning no more, and though a day seldom passed in which Elizabeth did not account for it clearly, there was little chance of her ever considering it with less perplexity. . .

Mr. Bennet treated the matter differently. . .

Let Wickham be your man. He is a pleasant fellow, and would jilt you creditably."

. . . Mr. Wickham's society was of material service in dispelling the gloom which the late perverse occurrences had thrown on many of the Longbourn family. They saw him often, and to his other recommendations was now added that of general unreserve. The whole of what Elizabeth had already heard, his claims on Mr. Darcy, and all that he had suffered from him, was now openly acknowledged and publicly canvassed; and everybody was pleased to know how much they had always disliked Mr. Darcy before they had known anything of the matter.

Miss Bennet was the only creature who could suppose there might be any extenuating circumstances in the case, unknown to the society of Hertfordshire; her mild and steady candor always pleaded for allowances, and urged the possibility of mistakes--but by everybody else Mr. Darcy was condemned as the worst of men.

*Whoever goes about slandering reveals secrets;
therefore do not associate with
a simple babbler.*
Proverbs 20:19

☙❧

A conversation about Elizabeth being the next daughter to be jilted, and by Wickham, caused her to reflect on the fact that nearly everyone in the neighborhood knew about Mr. Darcy's mistreatment of Wickham. No one questioned how the information came to be so openly known, or why it was only revealed after Darcy had left the neighborhood.

Only Jane questioned the story by saying that there must be factors that were simply not known about the case. Prejudice against Mr. Darcy made it easy for people to believe Wickham's story. May we be wiser than the people in Meryton for not believing every piece of gossip; may we take time to consider the circumstances and the source.

❧❧

After a week spent in professions of love and schemes of felicity, Mr. Collins was called from his amiable Charlotte by the arrival of Saturday. . .

On the following Monday, Mrs. Bennet had the pleasure of receiving her brother and his wife, who came as usual to spend the Christmas at Longbourn. Mr. Gardiner was a sensible, gentlemanlike man, greatly superior to his sister, as well by nature as education. . . Mrs. Gardiner, who was several years younger than Mrs. Bennet and Mrs. Phillips, was an amiable, intelligent, elegant woman, and a great favorite with all her Longbourn nieces. . .

The first of Mrs. Gardiner's business on her arrival was to distribute her presents and describe the newest fashions. When this was done she had a less active part to play. It became her turn to listen. . .

". . . Poor Jane! I am sorry for her, because, with her disposition, she may not get over it immediately. It had better have happened to *you*, Lizzy; you would have laughed yourself out of it sooner. But do you think she would be prevailed upon to go back with us? Change of scene might be of service--and perhaps a little relief from home may be as useful as anything." Elizabeth was exceedingly pleased with this proposal, and felt persuaded of her sister's ready acquiescence.

*Love one another with brotherly affection.
Outdo one another in showing honor.*
Romans 12:10

꙰

Mrs. Gardiner, who is wise and kind, observes the Bennet family, listens to accounts of recent events, and realizes her niece, Jane, needs some special attention. She feels that a change of locations will help remove Jane from the vicinity of painful memories and the foolishness of her mother's continual complaining. Mrs. Gardiner embodies the kind and affectionate relative who wisely cares for those she loves.

DAY SIXTY-TWO

❧❦

The Gardiners stayed a week at Longbourn; and what with the Phillipses, the Lucases, and the officers, there was not a day without its engagement. . . When the engagement was for home, some of the officers always made part of it--of which officers Mr. Wickham was sure to be one; and on these occasions, Mrs. Gardiner, rendered suspicious by Elizabeth's warm commendation, narrowly observed them both. Without supposing them, from what she saw, to be very seriously in love, their preference of each other was plain enough to make her a little uneasy; and she resolved to speak to Elizabeth on the subject before she left Hertfordshire, and represent to her the imprudence of encouraging such an attachment. . .

"You are too sensible a girl, Lizzy, to fall in love merely because you are warned against it; and, therefore, I am not afraid of speaking openly. Seriously, I would have you be on your guard. Do not involve yourself or endeavor to involve him in an affection which the want of fortune would make so very imprudent. I have nothing to say against him ; he is a most interesting young man; and if he had the fortune he ought to have, I should think you could not do better. But as it is, you must not let your fancy run away with you. You have sense, and we all expect you to use it. Your father would depend on your resolution and good conduct, I am sure. You must not disappoint your father."

". . . At present I am not in love with Mr. Wickham; no, I certainly am not. But he is, beyond all comparison, the most agreeable man I ever saw--and if he becomes really attached to me--I believe it will be better that he should not. I see the imprudence of it. Oh! that abominable Mr. Darcy! My father's opinion of me does me the greatest honor, and I should be miserable to forfeit it. . . All that I can promise you, therefore, is not to be in a hurry."

A good name is to be chosen rather than great riches, and favor is better than silver or gold.
Proverbs 22:1

Perhaps the opposite of many of today's situations, Elizabeth is being cautioned by her aunt against entering marriage for love only, without giving thought as to income. Elizabeth cherishes her father's good opinion of her wisdom and does not want to make him, or any member of her family, unhappy by making a rash decision. Many today will say, "You can't help falling in love; it just happens." Although commonly stated, it does not exemplify foresight. We enter many areas of life with great purpose; why shouldn't love and marriage have the same consideration? Elizabeth is choosing to adhere to the restrictions that come from protecting her reputation of being a wise woman.

DAY SIXTY-THREE

Mr. Collins returned into Hertfordshire soon after it had been quitted by the Gardiners and Jane; but as he took up his abode with the Lucases, his arrival was no great inconvenience to Mrs. Bennet. His marriage was now fast approaching, and she was at length so far resigned as to think it inevitable, and even repeatedly to say, in an ill-natured tone, that she "wished they might be happy." Thursday was to be the wedding day, and on Wednesday Miss Lucas paid her farewell visit; and when she rose to take leave, Elizabeth, ashamed of her mother's ungracious and reluctant good wishes, and sincerely affected herself, accompanied her out of the room. As they went downstairs together, Charlotte said,-

"I shall depend on hearing from you very often, Eliza."

"*That* you certainly shall."

"And I have another favor to ask you. Will you come and see me?"

"We shall often meet, I hope, in Hertfordshire."

"I am not likely to leave Kent for some time. Promise me, therefore, to come to Hunsford."

Elizabeth could not refuse, though she foresaw little pleasure in the visit.

"My father and Maria are coming to me in March," added Charlotte, "and I hope you will consent to be of the party. Indeed, Eliza, you will be as welcome as either of them."

Let marriage be held in honor among all...
Hebrews 13:4

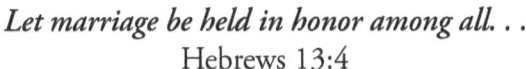

The wedding took place, and the bride and groom set off from the church. Elizabeth kept her promise and corresponded faithfully. Charlotte's letters were just like Mr. Collins' descriptions of the town, parsonage, gardens, and benefactress' mansion, just rationally softened. Her life soon fell into a routine, and Elizabeth looked forward to forming her own opinion upon her visit.

Although Charlotte chose to tolerate marriage with a fool in order to secure a living, and counted on Elizabeth's letters and visits to endure, she also chose honor. Charlotte's poor example aside, marriage is an honorable institution, a choice not to be made lightly. Mutual respect and love with a good dose of maturity is crucial to its success. Choose "honorable." Choose marriage.

DAY SIXTY-FOUR

☙❧

"My dearest Lizzy will, I am sure, be incapable of triumphing in her better judgement, at my expense, when I confess myself to have been entirely deceived in Miss Bingley's regard for me. But, my dear sister, though the event has proved you right, do not think me obstinate if I still assert that, considering what her behavior was, my confidence was as natural as your suspicion. . . I cannot understand it. If I were not afraid of judging harshly, I should be almost tempted to say that there is a strong appearance of duplicity in all this. But I will endeavor to banish every painful thought, and think only of what will make me happy--your affection, and the invariable kindness of my dear uncle and aunt. . ."

This letter gave Elizabeth some pain; but her spirits returned as she considered that Jane would no longer be duped, by the sister at least.

Let no one deceive you...
Ephesians 5:6

⁂

Jane finally realized that she had been deceived by Caroline Bingley's false friendship. Jane is experiencing the thought that truth hurts but chooses to remember that the truth can also set someone free. From the beginning, Elizabeth saw through the deception; something that Jane's good nature could not fathom. Jane relies on her love for her sister to help her through the pain of loss and learns the lessons of being the victim of deception.

DAY SIXTY-FIVE

❧❦

Mrs. Gardiner about this time reminded Elizabeth of her promise concerning that gentleman, and required information; and Elizabeth had such to send as might rather give contentment to her aunt than to herself. His apparent partiality had subsided, his attentions were over, he was the admirer of someone else. Elizabeth was watchful enough to see it all, but she could see it and write of it without material pain. Her heart had been but slightly touched, and her vanity was satisfied with believing that she would have been his only choice, had fortune permitted it. The sudden acquisition of ten thousand pounds was the most remarkable charm of the young lady to whom he was now rendering himself agreeable; but Elizabeth, less clear-sighted perhaps in this case than in Charlotte's, did not quarrel with him for his wish of independence. Nothing, on the contrary, could be more natural; and while able to suppose that it cost him a few struggles to relinquish her, she was ready to allow it a wise and desirable measure for both, and could very sincerely wish him happy. . .

". . . Importance may sometimes be purchased too dearly. Kitty and Lydia take his defection much more to heart than I do. They are young in the ways of the world, and not yet open to the mortifying conviction that handsome young men must have something to live on as well as the plain."

O Lord, who shall sojourn in your tent?
Who shall dwell on your holy hill?
He who walks blamelessly and does what is right
and speaks truth in his heart. . .
Psalm 15:1-2

❦

Elizabeth finds herself set aside by Mr. Wickham for a Miss King who had recently inherited ten thousand pounds. Wickham's affection for Elizabeth was light weight and easily swayed by the newly-acquired wealth of another. Elizabeth sees the situation, analyzes her own thoughts and emotions, and acknowledges that she was not truly in love with Wickham. Elizabeth's practice of speaking the truth to herself, protected her from being deeply wounded by Wickham's choice of money over her.

DAY SIXTY-SIX

AUTHOR'S SUMMARY OF EVENTS FROM PRIDE AND PREJUDICE:

Slowly January and February did pass. March was to take Elizabeth to Hunsford. Absence had increased her desire of seeing Charlotte again and had weakened her disgust of Mr. Collins. The only pain Elizabeth had of leaving her home was leaving her father, who would certainly miss her. He begged her to write and almost promised to answer her letters.

The farewell between her and Wickham was perfectly friendly.

The trip had been planned to include a stop in London to visit the Gardiners and Jane. The travelers started off without a problem the next day. Elizabeth endured her voyage companions. Sir William Lucas, and his daughter, Maria, a good-humored girl, but empty-headed as her father, had nothing to say worth hearing. Elizabeth listened to them with as much delight as the rattle of the coach.

Thankfully, the journey of only twenty-four miles to London, and the Gardiner's home on Gracechurch Street was quickly done. Jane and the family greeted them warmly. The day passed most pleasantly: the morning with shopping and bustle, and the evening at one of the theaters. Elizabeth contrived to sit by her aunt that evening, who said that although Jane struggled to support her spirits, there were periods of dejection. The conversation turned to Elizabeth's opinion of Wickham and his new love. Although Elizabeth claimed no pain, she confessed, "I am going near Mr. Wickham and Mr. Darcy's home in Derbyshire tomorrow. There I shall find a man, Mr. Collins, who has not one agreeable quality, who has neither manner, nor sense to recommend him. It seems that stupid men are the only ones worth knowing after all."

"Take care, Lizzy; that speech savors strongly of disappointment," her aunt responded. "How about you join your uncle and I on a trip this summer to the north country…we might go as far as the Lakes."

"What are men to rocks and mountains! I shall love to go," Elizabeth finished, ending the conversation with the anticipation of the joys of that trip.

*Strive for peace with everyone, and . . . see to it
. . .that no 'root of bitterness' springs up and
causes trouble . . .*
Hebrews 12:14-15

Although Elizabeth claims to not be wounded by Wickham's choice of Miss King or disgusted by Sir William Lucas and Mr. Collins and their folly, her speech shows bitterness. Jane, more sensitive, internalizes her disappointment and struggles with feelings of gloom. But Elizabeth, more practical and jaded, lets her hurt flow outward to accuse some of the men that she knows of foolishness. Jane attempts to follow peace with everyone, but Elizabeth needs to protect herself from the bitterness that is trying to creep into her soul.

DAY SIXTY-SEVEN

※

When they left the high road for the lane to Hunsford, every eye was in search of the Parsonage, and every turning expected to bring it in view. The palings of Rosings Park was their boundary on one side. Elizabeth smiled at the recollection of all that she had heard of its inhabitants.

At length the Parsonage was discernible. The garden sloping to the road, the house standing in it, the green pales, and the laurel hedge, everything declared they were arriving. Mr. Collins and Charlotte appeared at the door, and the carriage stopped at the small gate which led by a short gravel walk to the house, amidst the nods and smiles of the whole party. In a moment they were all out of the chaise, rejoicing at the sight of each other. Mrs. Collins welcomed her friend with the liveliest pleasure, and Elizabeth was more and more satisfied with coming when she found herself so affectionately received. She saw instantly that her cousin's manners were not altered by his marriage. . .

Elizabeth was prepared to see him in his glory; and she could not help in fancying that in displaying the good proportion of the room, its aspect and its furniture, he addressed himself particularly to her, as if wishing to make her feel what she had lost in refusing him. But though everything seemed neat and comfortable, she was not able to gratify him by any sigh of repentance, and rather looked with wonder at her friend that she could have so cheerful an air with such a companion.

Let another praise you, and not your own mouth;
a stranger, and not your own lips.
Proverbs 27:2

⁓⁕⁓

Elizabeth enjoyed her journey and her warm welcome from Charlotte but was disappointed to find that Mr. Collins was not positively altered by his marriage. Still an odd combination of false humility and pride, he sought to impress his guests, particularly Elizabeth, with the amazing wonders of his home. Mr. Collins was hoping Elizabeth was sorry that she had turned him down. His foolish nature pushed him to seek praise, but never waited for it, since he quickly complimented himself. Far from being sorry that she had not married Mr. Collins, Elizabeth was pleased to see her wise decision justified.

About the middle of the next day, as she was in her room getting ready for a walk, a sudden noise below seemed to speak the whole house in confusion; and, after listening a moment, she heard somebody running upstairs in a violent hurry, and calling loudly after her. She opened the door and met Maria in the landing place, who, breathless with agitation, cried out,--

"Oh, my dear Eliza! pray make haste and come into the dining-room, for there is such a sight to be seen! I will not tell you what it is. Make haste, and come down this moment. . ."

"And is this all?" cried Elizabeth. "I expected at least that the pigs were got into the garden, and here is nothing but Lady Catherine and her daughter."

"La! my dear," said Maria, quite shocked at the mistake, "it is not Lady Catherine. The old lady is Mrs. Jenkinson, who lives with them; the other is Miss de Bourgh. . ."

"She is abominably rude to keep Charlotte out of doors in all this wind. Why does she not come in?"

"Oh, Charlotte says she hardly ever does. It is the greatest of favors when Miss de Bourgh comes in. . ."

At length there was nothing more to be said; the ladies drove on, and the others returned into the house. Mr. Collins no sooner saw the two girls than he began to congratulate them on their good fortune, which Charlotte explained by letting them know that the whole party was asked to dine at Rosings the next day.

*...in humility count others more significant
than yourselves.*
Philippians 2:3

☙❧

Elizabeth's first glimpse of Miss De Bourgh on the next day was quickly followed by her first impression: Miss De Bourgh was rude, if only unintentionally, caused by an inbred self-centeredness. She thought nothing about keeping Charlotte standing out in the wind during a conversation. Rarely did Miss De Bourgh condescend to enter the parsonage. Elizabeth wisely understood that true greatness is always coupled with true humility and thoughtfulness.

DAY SIXTY-NINE

֎

Mr. Collins's triumph, in consequence of this invitation, was complete. The power of displaying the grandeur of his patroness to his wondering visitors, and of letting them see her civility towards himself and his wife, was exactly what he had wished for; and that an opportunity of doing it should be given so soon, was such an instance of Lady Catherine's condescension, as he knew not how to admire enough.

"I confess," said he, "that I should not have been at all surprised by her ladyship's asking us on Sunday to drink tea and spend the evening at Rosings. I rather expected, from my knowledge of her affability, that it would happen. But who could have foreseen such an attention as this? Who could have imagined that we should receive an invitation to dine there (an invitation, moreover, including the whole party) so immediately after your arrival!" . . .

"Do not make yourself uneasy, my dear cousin, about your apparel. Lady Catherine is far from requiring that elegance of dress in us which becomes herself and her daughter. I would advise you merely to put on whatever of your clothes is superior to the rest--there is no occasion for anything more. Lady Catherine will not think the worse of you for being simply dressed. She likes to have the distinction of rank preserved. . ."

When they ascended the steps to the hall, Maria's alarm was every moment increasing, and even Sir William did not look perfectly calm. Elizabeth's courage did not fail her. She had heard nothing of Lady Catherine that spoke her awful from any extraordinary talents or miraculous virtue, and the mere stateliness of money or rank she thought she could witness without trepidation.

. . . for they loved the glory that comes from man more than the glory that comes from God.
John 12:43

☙❧

Lady Catherine De Bourgh's pride caused her to desire that a distinction be kept between herself and others. She wanted her opulence to be admired. Mr. Collins' foolishness encouraged him to fall into line with Lady Catherine's way of thinking. Elizabeth felt, that because she had heard nothing spectacular concerning her Ladyship's character or talents to warrant such worship, that she could manage to witness the splendor with a calm heart. Her wise and independent spirit allowed her to rise to meet Lady Catherine on equal ground.

DAY SEVENTY

From the entrance-hall, of which Mr. Collins pointed out, with a rapturous air, the fine proportion and the finished ornaments, they followed the servants through an antechamber, to the room where Lady Catherine, her daughter, and Mrs. Jenkinson were sitting. Her ladyship, with great condescension, arose to receive them; and as Mrs. Collins had settled it with her husband that the office of introduction should be hers, it was performed in a proper manner, without any of those apologies and thanks which he would have thought necessary.

In spite of having been at St. James's Sir William was so completely awed by the grandeur surrounding him, that he had but just courage enough to make a very low bow, and take his seat without saying a word; and his daughter, frightened almost out of her senses, sat on the edge of her chair, not knowing which way to look. Elizabeth found herself quite equal to the scene, and could observe the three ladies before her composedly. Lady Catherine was a tall, large woman, with strongly-marked features, which might once have been handsome. Her air was not conciliating, nor was her manner of receiving them such as to make her visitors forget their inferior rank. . .

The dinner was exceedingly handsome, and there were all the servants and all the articles of plate which Mr. Collins had promised; and, as he had likewise foretold, he took his seat at the bottom of the table, by her ladyship's desire, and looked as if he felt that life could furnish nothing greater. . .

But Lady Catherine seemed gratified by their excessive admiration, and gave most gracious smiles, especially when any dish on the table proved a novelty to them.

For by the grace given to me I say to everyone among you not to think of himself more highly than he ought to think, but to think with sober judgment, each according to the measure of faith that God has assigned.
Romans 12:3

❧❦

Lady Catherine is the embodiment of the person who takes herself too seriously. A lifetime of poor training, mixed with pride over her rank and no one to oppose her, had created in her a spirit of self-importance. She loved to be admired and felt herself to be the authority on every subject. Paul reminds us to think humbly, not highly, of ourselves. True greatness is attached to the truth that each person is connected to the same human race. Each one is amazing because of the resilient spirit within, that was placed there by the Creator. Humanity's worth rests in Him.

DAY SEVENTY-ONE

When the ladies returned to the drawing-room, there was little to be done but to hear Lady Catherine talk, which she did without any intermission till coffee came in, delivering her opinion on every subject in so decisive a manner, as proved that she was not used to have her judgement controverted...

"Do you play and sing, Miss Bennet?"

"A little."

"...Do you draw?"

"No, not at all."

"What! None of you?...That is very strange... Has your governess left you?"

"We never had any governess."

"No governess!...I never heard of such a thing. Your mother must have been quite a slave to your education," Lady Catherine exclaimed. Elizabeth could hardly help smiling as she assured her that had not been the case...

"Are any of your younger sisters out [in society], Miss Bennet?"

"Yes, ma'am, all."

"All! What, all five out at once? Very odd! And you only the second. The younger ones out before the elder are married!"

". . .I think it would be very hard upon younger sisters, that they should not have their share of society and amusement, because the elder may not have the means or inclination to marry early. The last born has as good a right to pleasures of youth as the first."

"Upon my word," said her ladyship, "you give your opinion very decidedly for so young a person."

But let none of you suffer. . .as a meddler.
1 Peter 4:15

Lady Catherine, from her lofty opinion of herself, feels quite at home questioning Elizabeth on her family. She expresses shock over their lack of governess and the thought that all five sisters could be out in society at once. Elizabeth, whose confidence derives from wisdom and learning, answers each question nobly, eliciting expressions of shock from Lady Catherine. The Bible advises against being a busybody; against feeling as if we have a right to interfere in other people's matters. Each of us has enough to do keeping ourselves in line without becoming an authority in the details of others' lives.

DAY SEVENTY-TWO

❧❧

Sir William stayed only a week at Hunsford, but his visit was long enough to convince him of his daughter's being most comfortably settled, and of her possessing such a husband and such a neighbor as were not often met with. . .

Elizabeth had heard soon after her arrival that Mr. Darcy was expected there in the course of a few weeks, and though there were not many of her acquaintance whom she did not prefer, his coming would furnish one comparatively new to look at in their Rosings parties, and she might be amused in seeing how hopeless Miss Bingley's designs on him were, by his behavior to his cousin, for whom he was evidently destined by Lady Catherine, who talked of his coming with the greatest satisfaction, spoke of him in terms of the highest admiration, and seemed almost angry to find that he had already been frequently seen by Miss Lucas and herself. His arrival was soon known at the Parsonage; for Mr. Collins was walking the whole morning within view of the lodges opening into Hunsford Lane, in order to have the earliest assurance of it, and after making his bow as the carriage turned into the Park, hurried home with the great intelligence. On the following morning he hastened to Rosings to pay his respects. There were two nephews of Lady Catherine to require them, for Mr. Darcy had brought with him a Colonel Fitzwilliam, the younger son of his uncle Lord, and, to the great surprise of all the party, when Mr. Collins returned, the gentlemen accompanied him.

"I may thank you, Eliza, for this piece of civility. Mr. Darcy would never have come so soon to wait upon me."

. . .their approach was announced by the doorbell, and shortly afterwards the three gentlemen entered the room. Colonel Fitzwilliam, who led the way, was about thirty, not handsome, but in person and address most truly the gentleman.

Colonel Fitzwilliam entered into conversation directly with the readiness and ease of a well-bred man, and talked very pleasantly; but his cousin, after having addressed a slight observation on the house and garden to Mrs. Collins, sat for some time without speaking to anybody. At length, however, his civility was so far awakened as to inquire of Elizabeth after the health of her family. She answered him in the usual way, and after a moment's pause, added:

"My eldest sister has been in town these three months. Have you never happened to see her there?"

She was perfectly sensible that he never had; but she wished to see whether he would betray any consciousness of what had passed between the Bingleys and Jane, and she thought he looked a little confused as he answered that he had never been so fortunate as to meet Miss Bennet.

But let none of you suffer. . .as a meddler.
1 Peter 4:15

Elizabeth was pleased with her first meeting with Mr. Darcy's cousin, Colonel Fitzwilliam. His gentleman-like manner was pleasant, but Mr. Darcy was still reserved in his greeting, despite Charlotte's suggestion that he was making the visit so soon just to see Elizabeth. Partly from curiosity, partly from spite, Elizabeth questioned Mr. Darcy about his knowledge of Jane's being in London for three months. Although he denied knowing about Jane, his look of confusion seemed to indicate that he knew something. Had Elizabeth tripped onto some guilt that Mr. Darcy was hiding? The heart knows the depths of its own secrets.

Colonel Fitzwilliam's manners were very much admired at the parsonage, and the ladies felt that he must add considerably to their engagements at Rosings. It was some days, however, before they received any invitation thither--for while there were visitors in the house, they could not be necessary; and it was not till Easter-day . . .that they were honored by such an attention.

. . .Colonel Fitzwilliam seemed really glad to see them; anything was a welcome relief to him at Rosings; and Mrs. Collins's pretty friend had moreover caught his fancy very much. He now seated himself by her, and talked so agreeably. . . as to draw the attention of Lady Catherine herself, as well as of Mr. Darcy. His eyes had been soon and repeatedly turned towards them with a look of curiosity; and that her ladyship, after a while, shared the feeling, was more openly acknowledged, for she did not scruple to call out:

"What is that you are saying, Fitzwilliam? What is it you are talking of? What are you telling Miss Bennet? Let me hear what it is."

*God opposes the proud but gives grace
to the humble.*
1 Peter 4:15

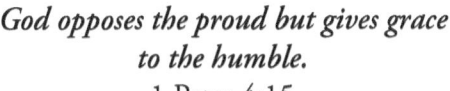

The difference in the personality and manners between Colonel Fitzwilliam and Mr. Darcy are marked. Fitzwilliam, a younger son and not an heir, has a less important position in life; he was raised with this knowledge. He chose military service and improved himself in wisdom, conversation, and general friendliness. He thought Elizabeth attractive and enjoyed talking with her. Darcy, the oldest in his family and heir to a large estate, was proudly raised to always remember the importance of his position. His good looks were not enhanced by a friendly attitude like that of Colonel Fitzwilliam. Fitzwilliam's sudden attraction to Elizabeth draws his attention. Pride and humility are both evident. Pride from Darcy; humility and genuineness from Fitzwilliam. Grace is Fitzwilliam's adornment, which is lacking in Darcy.

When coffee was over, Fitzwilliam reminded Elizabeth of having promised to play for him; and she sat down directly to the instrument. He drew a chair near her. Lady Catherine listened to half a song, and then talked as before, to her other nephew; till the latter walked away from her, and moving with his usual deliberation towards the pianoforte, stationed himself so as to command a full view of her the fair performer's countenance. . .

"You mean to frighten me, Mr. Darcy, by coming in all this state to hear me."

"I shall not say that you are mistaken," he replied, "because you cannot really believe me to entertain any design of alarming you; and I have had the pleasure of your acquaintance long enough to know that you find great enjoyment in occasionally professing opinions which in fact are not your own."

Elizabeth laughed heartily at this picture of herself. . ."It is provoking me to retaliate, and such things may come out as will shock your relations to hear."

"I am not afraid of you," said he, smilingly.

"Fitzwilliam, you shall hear then--but prepare yourself for something very dreadful. The first time of my ever seeing him in Hertfordshire . . .he danced only four dances, though gentlemen were scarce; and, to my certain knowledge, more than one young lady was sitting in want of a partner. . ."

"I did not at that time have the honor of knowing any lady in the assembly beyond my own party. . .I am ill-qualified to recommend myself to strangers. . . I certainly have not the talent of conversing easily with those I have never seen before."

"My fingers," said Elizabeth, "do not move over this instrument in the masterly manner which I see so many women's do. They have not the same force or rapidity, and do not produce the same expression. But then I have always supposed it to be my own fault--because I would not take the trouble of practicing. It is not that I do not believe *my* fingers as capable as any other woman's of superior execution."

Darcy smiled and said, "You are perfectly right. . .neither of us perform to strangers."

~~~

The plans of the diligent lead surely to abundance, but everyone who is hasty comes only to poverty.
Proverbs 21:5

~~~

This exchange between Darcy and Elizabeth is very transparent. Darcy claims to be too shy to converse easily with new acquaintances, implying that it is a lack of talent. When Colonel Fitzwilliam confesses that he believes his cousin is simply too proud to care, Elizabeth adds that anyone can practice until they become proficient or comfortable in an area. Often someone will lay blame to a weakness as something natural that they inherited, but Proverbs implies that diligent thinking and planning can lead to success. Elizabeth also believes Darcy to simply not care enough to practice his social skills, that he is too proud. Perhaps we should look at weaknesses as challenges, areas that can be improved through diligent practice.

DAY SEVENTY-FIVE

~~~

Elizabeth was sitting by herself the next morning, and writing to Jane, while Mrs. Collins and Maria were gone on business into the village, when she was startled by a ring at the door. . .and, to her very great surprise, Mr. Darcy, and Mr. Darcy only, entered the room. . .

[Elizabeth spoke,] "I think that I have understood that Mr. Bingley does not have much of an idea of returning to Netherfield again?"

"I have never heard him say so. . . This seems a very comfortable house. . . And Mr. Collins appears very fortunate in his choice of a wife."

"Yes, indeed. . . My friend has an excellent understanding--though I am not certain that I consider her marrying Mr. Collins as the wisest thing she ever did. She seems perfectly happy, however, and in prudential light it is certainly a very good match for her."

"It must be very agreeable to her to be settled within so easy a distance of her own family and friends."

". . .It is nearly fifty miles. . . I should never have considered the distance as one of the *advantages* oof the match," cried Elizabeth. . . "I do not mean to say that a woman may not be settled too near her family. The far and the near must be relative, and depend on the many varying circumstances."

. . .Mr. Darcy drew his chair a little towards her, and said, "*You* cannot have a right to such very strong local attachment. *You* cannot have been always at Longbourn."

Elizabeth looked surprised. The gentlemen experienced some change of feeling; he drew back his chair. . .

A short dialogue. . .soon put an end to by the entrance of Charlotte and her sister, just returned from their walk. . . Mr. Darcy. . .after sitting a few minutes longer without saying much to anybody, went away.

"What can be the meaning of this?" said Charlotte, as soon as he was gone. "My dear Eliza he must be in love with you, or he would never have called on us in this familiar way."

⁂

Little children, let us not love in word or talk but in deed and in truth.
1 John 3:18

⁂

Elizabeth denied such an explanation, but Mr. Darcy and Colonel Fitzwilliam called often to the parsonage after that. Sometimes together, sometimes separately. Charlotte was suspicious of Mr. Darcy's being partial to Elizabeth. But Elizabeth always countered the idea, saying that the men were merely bored with their stay at Rosings.

Mr. Darcy's frequent visits to the parsonage aroused Charlotte's suspicions that he was in love with Elizabeth, but his conversations said otherwise. He would often sit ten minutes without saying a word. It is a case of Mr. Darcy's actions speaking louder than his words he or lack thereof. When that first conversation turned to the distance between a married woman and her family, Elizabeth blushed. She believed that Darcy was thinking that Bingley and Jane being married, and living at Netherfield, was too close to her family. There are times when the words that are not spoken are louder than the ones that are.

DAY SEVENTY-SIX

❦

"Oh! yes," said Elizabeth dryly; "Mr. Darcy is uncommonly kind to Mr. Bingley, and takes a prodigious deal of care of him."

"Care of him! Yes, I really believe Darcy *does* take care of him. . . I have reason to think Bingley very much indebted to him. . . What he told me was merely this: that he congratulated himself on having lately saved a friend from the inconveniences of a most imprudent marriage, but without mentioning names or any other particulars and I only suspected it to be Bingley. . ."

"Did Mr. Darcy give you his reasons for this interference?"

"I understood that there were some very strong objections against the lady."

. . . Elizabeth made no answer, and walked on, her heart swelling with indignation. . .til they reached the parsonage. There, shut into her own room, as soon as their visitor left them, she could think without interruption of all that she had heard. . .

The agitation and tears which the subject occasioned, brought on a headache; and it grew so much worse towards the evening, that, added to her unwillingness to see Mr. Darcy, it determined her not to attend her cousins to Rosings where they were engaged to drink tea.

And he said to his disciples, 'Temptations to sin are sure to come, but woe to the one through whom they come!'
Luke 17:1

☙❧

Mr. Darcy had taken it upon himself to interfere in the relationship of Charles Bingley and Elizabeth's sister, Jane. Elizabeth had always supposed that Miss Bingley was the principle one to blame in taking Bingley away from Jane, but the information from Colonel Fitzwilliam had convinced Elizabeth that Mr. Darcy held the greater influence. The prejudice that she had always felt against Darcy was swelling into anger and a near hatred. Jesus noted that it is impossible to go through this world without encountering hurts and offenses, but laid responsibility on the one who offends. Mr. Darcy's pride and officious manner moved him to separate two people in love and caused Jane deep pain. Whether one is the offended or the offender, only humble apologies and forgiveness can be applied to remedy the hurt.

DAY SEVENTY-SEVEN

※

When they were gone, Elizabeth, as if intending to exasperate herself as much as possible against Mr. Darcy, chose for her employment the examination of all the letters which Jane had written to her. . . Mr. Darcy's shameful boast of what misery he had been able to inflict gave her a keener sense of her sister's sufferings.

. . .she was suddenly roused by the sound of the doorbell, and her spirits were a little fluttered by the idea of its being Colonel Fitzwilliam himself. . . But this idea was soon banished. . .when, to her utter amazement, she saw Mr. Darcy walk into the room. . .

"In vain have I struggled. It will not do. My feelings will not be repressed. You must allow me to tell you how ardently I admire and love you."

Elizabeth's astonishment was beyond expression. She stared, colored, doubted, and was silent. This he considered sufficient encouragement. . . He spoke well; but there were feelings besides those of the heart to be detailed, and he was not more eloquent on the subject of tenderness than of pride. His sense of her inferiority--of its being a degradation--of the family obstacles which judgment had always opposed to inclination, were dwelt on with a warmth which seemed due to the consequence he was wounding, but was very unlikely to recommend his suit.

. . . As he said this, she could easily see that he had no doubt of a favorable answer. . .and, when he ceased, the color rose into her cheeks, and she said,-

". . . I believe, the established mode to express a sense of obligation for the sentiments avowed, however unequally they may be returned. It is natural that obligation should be felt, and if I could *feel* gratitude, I would now thank you. But I cannot--I have never desired your good opinion, and you have certainly bestowed it most unwillingly. I am sorry to have occasioned pain to anyone. It has been most unconsciously done, however, and I hope will be of a short duration. . ."

"And this is all the reply which I am to have the honor of expecting! I might, perhaps, wish to be informed why, with so little endeavor at civility, I am thus rejected!"

A man's gift makes room for him and brings him before the great.
Proverbs 18:16

One could feel some pity for poor Mr. Darcy being rejected so decisively, if he had not approached his proposal to Elizabeth with so much arrogance. Once his initial expression of ardent love was complete, he proceeded to justify his doubts and struggles concerning the inferiority of Elizabeth's family connections. Instead of being a gentleman and hiding his misgivings, he let Elizabeth know that he was lowering himself to even propose. His haughty spirit was the last straw for Elizabeth, whose regret at having to say no, was quickly followed by justification of rejecting him so completely. His pride has led to his fall.

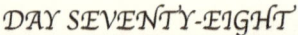

"I might as well inquire," replied she, "why with so evident a design of offending and insulting me, you chose to tell me that you like me against your will, against your reason, and even against your character? Was not this some excuse for uncivility, if I *was* uncivil? But I have other provocations. You know I have. Had not my own feelings decided against you--had they been indifferent, or had they even been favorable, do you think that any consideration would tempt me to accept the man who has been the means of ruining, perhaps forever, the happiness of a most beloved sister?"

As she pronounced these words, Mr. Darcy changed color; but the emotion was short, and he listened without attempting to interrupt her while she continued. . .

"Can you deny that you have done it?"

"I have no wish of denying that I did everything in my power to separate my friend from your sister, or that I rejoice in my success. Towards *him* I have been kinder than towards myself."

Blessed is the one who fears the Lord always,
but whoever hardens his heart
will fall into calamity.
Proverbs 28:14

❦

An immediate response of remorse or repentance from Mr. Darcy could have significantly altered his current conversation with Elizabeth. It is always better to be overly careful to not hurt or offend someone in the first place. But Mr. Darcy went so far as to harden his heart and excuse the wound that he had inflicted both on his friend and Jane. Let us always be prepared to push the reset button of humility and seek forgiveness, rather than harden our hearts and pridefully excuse an offense.

"But it is not merely this affair," she continued, "on which my dislike is founded. Long before it had taken place, my opinion of you was decided. Your character was unfolded in the recital which I received many months ago from Mr. Wickham. On this subject, what can you have to say?"

"You take an eager interest in that gentleman's concerns," Mr. Darcy said in a less tranquil tone, and with heightened color.

"Who that knows what his misfortunes have been, can help feeling an interest in him?"

"His misfortunes!" repeated Darcy contemptuously; "yes, his misfortunes have been great indeed."

"And of your infliction," cried Elizabeth with energy. "You have reduced him to his present state of poverty-comparative poverty. . . and yet you can treat the mention of his misfortunes with contempt and ridicule."

"And this," cried Darcy, as he walked with quick steps across the room, "is your opinion of me! But perhaps," added he, stopping in his walk, and turning towards her, "these offenses might have been overlooked, had not your pride been hurt by my honest confession of the scruples that had long prevented my forming any serious design. . . Could you expect me to rejoice in the inferiority of your connections?--to congratulate myself on the hope of relations, whose condition in life is so decidedly beneath my own?"

"You are mistaken, Mr. Darcy, if you suppose that the mode of your declaration affected me in any other way, than as it spared me the concern which I might have felt in refusing you, had you behaved in a more gentleman-like manner."

She saw him start at this, but he said nothing, and she continued, "You could not have made me the offer of your hand in any possible way that would have tempted me to accept it. . . From the very beginning--from the first moment, I may almost say--of my acquaintance with you, your manners, impressing me with the fullest belief of your arrogance, your conceit, and your self disdain of the feelings of others, were such as to form that groundwork of disapprobation on which succeeding events have built so immovable a dislike; and I had not known you a month before I felt that you were the last man in the world whom I could ever be prevailed on to marry."

"You have said quite enough, madam. I perfectly comprehend your feelings, and have now only to be ashamed of what my own have been. Forgive me for having taken up so much of your time, and accept my wishes for your health and happiness."

Rather, speaking the truth in love, we are to grow up in every way into him who is the head, into Christ.
Ephesians 4:15

This scene fully reveals the purpose of the title: pride and conceit on the part of Mr. Darcy, and prejudice on the part of Elizabeth. Mr. Darcy made it clear that he felt that he was lowering himself to propose to Elizabeth because of her family connections. Elizabeth began with a dislike for Mr. Darcy, that was fanned into contempt by Mr. Wickham's tale, then into a near disgust by knowledge of Darcy's involvement in Jane's misery. The two were speaking the truth, but not tempering it with love. Only humble and transparent honesty could remedy the rift between Elizabeth and Mr. Darcy.

DAY EIGHTY

"I have been walking in the grove sometime in hope of meeting you. Will you do me the honor of reading that letter?" he asked. . .

With no expectation of pleasure, but the strongest curiosity, Elizabeth opened the letter, and, to her still increasing wonder, perceived an envelope containing two sheets of letter paper, written quite through, in a very close hand. . . It was dated from Rosings, at eight o'clock in the morning. . .

"Be not alarmed, madam, on receiving this letter by apprehension of its containing. . .a renewal of offers, which last night were so disgusting to you. . . Two offenses of a very different nature, and by no means of equal magnitude, you last night laid to my charge. . ."

A friend loves at all times...
Proverbs 17:17

And as you wish that others would do to you,
do so to them.
Luke 6:31

☙❧

Knowing Mr. Darcy's character, it is not surprising that he feels justified in his actions concerning separating Bingley and Jane. Darcy feels as if he is being a true friend by preventing Bingley from entering a marriage that would bring him shame, especially as it related to the Bennet family and their lack of propriety. But if the roles were reversed, Mr. Darcy would consider Bingley to be officiously interfering. Mr. Darcy's love for his friend should have been tempered by the golden rule: remembering to do to others as you would have them do to you. Some would say that Mr. Darcy's behavior in this situation was motivated by concern for his friend, others may claim that his own pride was the prevailing factor. Darcy would certainly not wish to be a part of Bingley's life, if Bingley was a part of Jane's.

DAY EIGHTY-ONE

☙❧

"With respect to the other, more weighty accusation, of having injured Mr. Wickham, I can only refute it by laying before you the whole of his connection with my family. . . Mr. Wickham is the son of a very respectable man, who had for many years the management of all the Pemberley estates, and whose good conduct. . .inclined my father to be of service to him; and on George Wickham, who was his godson, his kindness was therefore liberally bestowed. . .

"My excellent father died about five years ago; and his attachment to Mr. Wickham was to the last so steady, that in his will he particularly recommended it to me, to promote his advancement in the best manner that his profession might allow. . . I thought to ill of him to invite him to Pemberley, or admit his society in town. . .
But last summer he again most painfully obtruded on my notice. . .

"...he so far recommended himself to Georgiana, whose affectionate heart retained a strong impression of his kindness to her as a child, that she was persuaded to believe herself in love, and to consent to an elopement. She was then but fifteen. . . I am happy to add, joined them unexpectedly. . .and then Georgiana. . . acknowledged the whole to me. You may imagine what I felt and how I acted. . . Mr. Wickham's chief object was unquestionably my sister's fortune, which is thirty thousand pounds; and I cannot help but supposing that the hope of revenging himself on me was a strong inducement. His revenge would have been complete

He frustrates the devices of the crafty,
so that their hands achieve no success.
Job 5:12

❧

Mr. Wickham's true character is laid out bare, for Elizabeth to see. Although his well-practiced manners had convinced her that he had been financially destroyed, the truth shows that his foolish choices and evil intentions brought about his own destruction. God Himself is often the whistleblower. He disappoints the evil plans of the wicked by letting their character be exposed: to the ridicule of the world, and the rejoicing of the righteous. The truth shows that Mr. Darcy's tolerance of Wickham in Hertfordshire was noble…he allowed Wickham to move through that neighborhood's society without exposing him as the fraud he was. If we are devious, let us be aware of God, the One who disappoints wicked plans. If we are the victim, take hope in the reward of the wicked. God is in control.

DAY EIGHTY-TWO

❧❦

With a strong prejudice against everything that he might have to say, she began his account of what had happened at Netherfield . . . The worst objections to the match, made her too angry to have any wish of doing him justice. He expressed no regret for what he had done which satisfied her; his style his style was not penitent but haughty.

But when this subject was succeeded by his account of Mr. Wickham. . .her feelings were yet more acutely painful and more difficult of definition. . .and when she had gone through the whole letter, though scarcely knowing anything of the last page or two, put it hastily away, protesting that she would not regard it, that she would never look in it again.

In half a minute the letter was unfolded again, and. . .she again began the mortifying perusal of all that related to Wickham, and comanded herself so far as to examine the meaning of every sentence.

She perfectly remembered everything that had passed in conversation between Wickham and herself, in their first evening at Mr. Philips's. . . She was *now* struck with the impropriety of such communications to a stranger, and wondered it had escaped her before.

. . . She grew absolutely ashamed of herself. . . "How despicably have I acted!" she cried; "I who have prided myself on my discernment! I, who have valued myself on my abilities. . . How humiliating in this discovery! yet, how just a humiliation!"

. . . Widely different was the effect of a second perusal.

For I know my transgressions,
and my sin is ever before me.
Psalm 51:3

Behold, you delight in truth in the inward being,
and you teach me wisdom in the secret heart.
Psalm 51:6

☙❧

Initially, Elizabeth allowed her prejudice against Mr. Darcy to foment her anger as she read the letter. She determined to put it away and never peruse it again, but her honest spirit would not let her leave it alone. After careful thought, she came to see the hypocrisy in Mr. Wickham's words and actions. She thought that it was strange that she had not noticed that imprudence at the beginning. Finally, she was forced to accept first the truth about herself, then the truth concerning Mr. Darcy's side of the Wickham story. Elizabeth acknowledged that her vanity, her pride in her powers of discernment, had caused her to quickly accept Wickham's version of his relationship with Darcy. Truth always has the ability to set a person free, and truth spoken to one's own heart, can free that person from the confines of both pride and prejudice.

DAY EIGHTY-THREE

❧❦

From herself to Jane--from Jane to Bingley, her thoughts were in a line which soon brought to her recollection that Mr. Darcy's explanation *there* had appeared very insufficient. . . He declared himself to have been totally unsuspicious of her sister's attachment; and she could not help remembering what Charlotte's opinion had always been. . . Jane's feelings, though fervent, were little displayed, and that there was a constant complacency in her air and manner not often united with great sensibility.

When she came to that part of the letter in which her family were mentioned in terms of such mortifying, yet merited reproach, her sense of shame was severe. . .and as she considered that Jane's disappointment had in fact been the work of her nearest relations. . .she felt depressed beyond anything she had ever known before.

After wandering the along the land for two hours. . .fatigue, and a recollection of her long absence, made her at length return home; and she entered the house with the wish of appearing cheerful as usual. . .

She was immediately told that the two gentlemen from Rosings had each called during her absence; Mr. Darcy, only for a few minutes to take leave, but that Colonel Fitzwilliam had been sitting with them at least an hour, hoping for her return. . . Colonel Fitzwilliam was no longer an object. She could think only of her letter.

But the one who did not know, and did what deserved a beating, will receive a light beating. Everyone to whom much was given, of him much will be required, and from him to whom they entrusted much, they will demand the more.
Luke 12:48

By concluding that Mr. Darcy was telling the truth concerning Wickham, Elizabeth decided to reread the account of Jane and Bingley with a more open mind. She had to accept, though deeply painful, the truth about her family. And the idea that Jane's broken heart was caused by her own relatives, made Elizabeth feel heavy and depressed. Although truth can free from the weight of deception, it can also add the weight of responsibility. What would Elizabeth do with her new knowledge?

DAY EIGHTY-FOUR

Reflection must be reserved for solitary hours; whenever she was alone, she gave way to it as the greatest relief; and not a day went by without a solitary walk, in which she might indulge in all the delight of unpleasant recollections.

Mr. Darcy's letter she was in a fair way of soon knowing by heart. She studied every sentence; and her feelings toward its writer were at times widely different. When she remembered the style of his address, she was still full of indignation but when she considered how unjustly she had condemned and upbraided him, her anger was turned against herself; and his disappointed feelings became the object of compassion. His attachment excited gratitude, his general character respect...

Good sense wins favor...
Proverbs 13:15

❦

Elizabeth's reflections on the letter, Mr. Darcy's proposal, and the obvious flaws of her family, began to change her opinion of herself and Mr. Darcy. Her complete understanding of the situation, as revealed by careful study of the letter, moved her to feel compassion for Mr. Darcy and the wound she must have caused him. Elizabeth may not have been fully aware of the changes within her but being brutally honest with oneself is a positive step toward a new way of thinking. A fresh perspective can influence a person's attitude, opinions, and eventually their actions.

DAY EIGHTY-FIVE

––

On Saturday morning, Elizabeth and Mr. Collins met for breakfast a few minutes before the others appeared. . .

". . .let me assure you, my dear Miss Elizabeth, that I can from my heart most cordially wish you equal felicity in marriage. My dear Charlotte and I have but one mind and one way of thinking. There is in everything a most remarkable resemblance of character and ideas between us. We seem to have been designed for each other."

. . . Poor Charlotte! it is melancholy to leave her to such society! But she had chosen in with her eyes open. . .she did not seem to ask for compassion.

. . . At length the chaise arrived. . .and it was pronounced to be read . . .the door was then allowed to be shut and the carriage drove off.

"Good gracious!" cried Maria. . . "It seems but a day or two since we first came!--and yet how many things have happened! . . . How much I shall have to tell!"

Elizabeth privately added, "And how much I shall have to conceal!"

*The wisdom of the prudent is to discern his way,
but the folly of fools is deceiving.*
Proverbs 13:15

༄༅༄

Although Elizabeth's time at Hunsford had caused her to take a long, honest look at herself, sadly no such progress could be seen in Mr. Collins. Was Mr. Collins blinded by hypocrisy, foolishness, or pride? He was certainly arrogant in assuming that he was the perfect catch. And he was arrogant in assuming that Charlotte agreed with him on everything. Shakespeare said, "To thine own self be true." Mr. Collins seems to be a hopeless case where everyone knows how foolish he is except himself.

But Elizabeth is growing in wisdom as she is growing in speaking honestly with herself.

DAY EIGHTY-SIX

❧❦

After welcoming their sisters, they triumphantly displayed a table set out with such cold meat as an inn larder usually affords. . . "Is this not nice? is not this an agreeable surprise? And we mean to treat you all," added Lydia; "but you must lend us the money, for we have just spent ours at the shop out there."

. . . As soon as all had eaten. . .the carriage was ordered; and after some contrivance, the whole party, with. . .the unwelcome addition of Kitty's and Lydia's purchases, were seated in it.

"How nicely we are crammed in," cried Lydia. "I am glad I bought my bonnet, if it is only for the fun of having another band box!"

. . . With such kind histories of their parties and good jokes, did Lydia. . .endeavor to amuse her companions all the way to Longbourne.

*Know this, my beloved brothers: let every person be
quick to hear, slow to speak, slow to anger...*
James 1:19

☙❧

Lydia's character was so self-absorbed that she seldom thought of anyone beyond herself. The return of the older sisters to Longbourn should have been a delight for everyone, but the girls had little opportunity to share stories from their respective trips because of Lydia. Lydia's foolish habits were only laughed at by her father and encouraged by her mother. Asking questions and listening attentively to the answers are a reflection of an understanding heart, one that Lydia simply does not possess. Listening leads to knowledge and eventually wisdom: a practice the youngest Bennet sister desperately needed to acquire.

DAY EIGHTY-SEVEN

❧

Elizabeth's impatience to acquaint Jane with what had happened could no longer be overcome. . .she related to her the next morning the chief of the scenes between Mr. Darcy and herself. Miss Bennet's astonishment was soon lessened. . . She was sorry that Mr. Darcy should have delivered his sentiments in a manner so little suited to recommend them; but still more was she grieved for the unhappiness which her sister's refusal must have given him. . .

"Indeed," replied Elizabeth, "I am heartily sorry for him; but he has other feelings, which will probably soon drive away his regard for me. You do not blame me, however, for refusing him?"

"Blame you! Oh, no!"

"But you blame me for having spoken so warmly of Wickham?"

"No--I do not know that you were wrong in saying what you did."

"But you *will* know it, when I have told you what happened the very next day."

". . . Poor Wickham! there is such an expression of goodness in his countenance!"

". . . There certainly was some great mismanagement in the education of those two young men. One has got all the goodness, and the other all the appearance of it."

*But what comes out of the mouth
proceeds from the heart...*
James 1:19

❦

Elizabeth told Jane about Darcy's letter, concerning George Wickham. Poor Jane: she would have willingly gone through the world without believing that there was so much wickedness in the whole race of mankind, as were here collected in one individual, George Wickham.

Jane is initially shocked by Mr. Darcy's proposal, but more so by the truth concerning Mr. Wickham's character. She pities Mr. Darcy for being so sure of Elizabeth's positive answer, and for being rejected so soundly. But Elizabeth's accusation of Darcy's mistreatment of Wickham makes Jane cringe.

Elizabeth confessed that the prejudice in her heart led her to trust Wickham and malign Darcy, even to his face. Her prejudice fostered bitterness which led to verbal accusations against the one person most affected by Wickham's evil character.

DAY EIGHTY-EIGHT

⁂

The first week of their return was soon gone. The second began. It was the last of the regiment's stay in Meryton, and all the young ladies in the neighborhood were drooping apace... The elder Miss Bennets alone were still able to eat, drink, and sleep, and pursue the usual course of their employments. Very frequently were they reproached for this insensibility by Kitty and Lydia, whose own misery was extreme...

But the gloom of Lydia's prospect was shortly cleared away; for she received an invitation from Mrs. Forster...to accompany her to Brighton... Lydia flew about the house in restless ecstasy, calling for everyone's congratulations... whilst the luckless Kitty continued in the parlor repining at her fate...

"If you were aware," said Elizabeth, "of the very great disadvantage to us all which much arise from the public notice of Lydia's unguarded and imprudent manner...I am sure you would judge differently in the affair."

... Mr. Bennet saw that her whole heart was in the subject, and affectionately taking her hand, said in reply-

"Do not make yourself uneasy, my love... We shall have no peace at Longbourn if Lydia does not go to Brighton."

The prudent sees danger and hides himself,
but the simple go on and suffer for it.
Proverbs 22:3

※

Elizabeth sees the impending doom that would likely result from Lydia's getting exactly what she always wanted: an opportunity to flirt shamelessly without her family's oversight. Her attempt to advise her father to check Lydia's behavior before it becomes a lifelong habit fell on deaf ears. Mr. Bennet prizes the peace of letting Lydia have her way over the struggle needed to protect her from herself. He believes that Elizabeth is overexaggerating the damage that Lydia's foolishness can have on the reputation of the other sisters. Being prudent, looking into the future, and trying to avoid pain or damage is worth any effort. It is much easier to prevent a problem than to fix one!

DAY EIGHTY-NINE

❦

On the very last day, [Wickham] dined with others of the officers, at Longbourn; and so little was Elizabeth disposed to part from him in good humor, that on his making some inquiry as to the manner in which her time has passed at Hunsford, she mentioned Colonel Fitzwilliam's and Mr. Darcy's having both spent three weeks at Rosings, and asked him if he was acquainted with the former.

He looked surprised, displeased, alarmed; but with a moment's recollection and a returning smile, replied that he had formerly seen him often. . .

"His manners are very different from his cousin's."

"Yes, very different. But I think Mr. Darcy improves on acquaintance."

"Indeed!" cried Wickham, with a look which did not escape her. . . "Is it in address that he improves. . .for I dare not hope. . .that he is improved in essentials."

"Oh, no!" said Elizabeth. "In essentials, I believe, he is very much whatever he was. . .when I said that he improved on acquaintance . . .from knowing him better, his disposition was better understood."

Wickham's alarm now appeared in a heightened complexion and agitated look; for a few minutes he was silent. . .shaking off his embarrassment. . .

She saw that he wanted to engage her on the old subject of his grievances, and she was in no humor to indulge him.

*The wicked flee when no one pursues,
but the righteous are bold as a lion.*
Proverbs 28:1

≈≈

Elizabeth, now confident in her knowledge of Wickham's true character, confronts him at a final dinner party together. She toys with his self-importance by mentioning that she met and frequently talked with Colonel Fitzwilliam during her visit with Charlotte. She then boldly states that she met almost daily with both Fitzwilliam and Mr. Darcy. Wickham quickly lost his brazen demeanor and became the prey in the hands of the hunter. Elizabeth even went so far as to state that her opinion of Mr. Darcy had improved upon knowing him better. Unable to defend himself without exposing himself, Wickham slipped into silence and simply ignored Elizabeth for the rest of the evening. Wickham's willingness to retreat from his conversation with Elizabeth was merely a confirmation of his guilty conscience, and Elizabeth's boldness to coyly confront him is based upon her knowledge of the truth concerning him. Nothing adds strength like the truth and a clear conscience to pursue the truth.

Had Elizabeth's opinion been all drawn from her own family, she could not have formed a very pleasing picture of conjugal felicity or domestic comfort. Her father, captivated by youth and beauty, and that appearance of good humor which youth and beauty generally give, had married a woman whose weak understanding and illiberal mind had very early in their marriage put an end to all real affection for her. Respect, esteem, and confidence had vanished forever; and all his views of domestic happiness were overthrown. But Mr. Bennet was not of a disposition to seek comfort for the disappointment which his own imprudence had brought on. . . To his wife he was very little otherwise indebted, than as her ignorance and folly had contributed to his amusement.

Elizabeth, however, had never been blind to the impropriety of her father's behavior as a husband. . .but respecting his abilities, and grateful for his affectionate treatment of herself. . .she endeavored to forget what she could not overlook. . . But she had never felt so strongly as now the disadvantages which must attend the children of so unsuitable a marriage.

Strength and dignity are her clothing,
and she laughs at the time to come.
She opens her mouth with wisdom,
and the teaching of kindness is on her tongue.
Proverbs 31:25-26

❧✥

Mr. Bennet's mistake of marrying a weak-minded woman led him to openly disrespect her in front of his children. His wife's folly became the source of his amusement. Mrs. Bennet, the opposite of the ideal woman in Proverbs 31, is only self-centered and foolish. She brings an empty head to both her marriage and her mothering. Elizabeth not only bemoans the lack of respect in her parents' marriage, but she also feels discouraged about the ways it has affected her sisters. If her father was to gain no joy from being tied to a foolish woman, he could have at least taken the responsibility of making sure that his daughters did not follow their mother's example. One poor choice does not need to birth a lifetime of poor choices.

The time fixed for the beginning of their northern tour was now fast approaching. . .when a letter arrived from Mrs. Gardiner, which at once delayed its commencement and curtailed its extent. . .

Elizabeth was excessively disappointed. . .but it was her business to be satisfied--and certainly her temper to be happy; and all was soon right again.

With the mention of Derbyshire there were many ideas connected. It was impossible for her to see the word without thinking of Pemberley and its owner.

One enjoyment was certain--that of suitableness as companions; a suitableness which comprehended health and temper to bear inconveniences--cheerfulness to enhance every pleasure--and affection and intelligence, which might supply it among themselves if there were disappointments abroad.

Iron sharpens iron,
and one man sharpens another.
Proverbs 27:17

The disappointment of the delayed and curtailed trip was soon forgotten as Elizabeth and her aunt and uncle began to enjoy their journey together. Their balanced personalities and ways of thinking were similar, creating a positive environment for absorbing every pleasure from their vacation together. Similar spirits can only enhance the joy of sharing an adventure. That Elizabeth found herself in a position to worry about the part of their trip that would take them on a tour of Pemberley mansion; it was a distress that she would have to bear alone. Her family was unaware of the proposal that she had refused from Pemberley's owner. Her aunt and uncle eagerly anticipated the opportunity to see the grounds and home, while Elizabeth worried about a chance encounter with Mr. Darcy.

DAY NINETY-TWO

❧❧

Elizabeth, as they drove along, watched for the first appearance of Pemberley Woods. . .when at length they turned in at the lodge, her spirits were in a high flutter. . . Elizabeth was delighted. She had never seen a place for which nature had done more. . .

"I have heard much of your master's fine person," said Mrs. Gardiner. . . "It is a handsome face. But, Lizzy, you can tell us whether it is lie or not."

". . . Does that young lady know Mr. Darcy?"

Elizabeth colored, and said, "A little."

"And do not you think him a very handsome gentleman, ma'am?"

"Yes, very handsome."

"He is the best landlord and the best master. . .that ever lived. . . There is not one of his tenants or servants but what will give him a good name. Some people call him proud; but I am sure I never saw anything of it. . ."

The commendation bestowed on him by Mrs. Reynolds was of no trifling nature. What praise is more valuable than the praise of an intelligent servant. . . Every idea that had been brought forward by the housekeeper was favorable to his character, and as [Elizabeth] stood before the canvas on which he was represented. . .she thought of his regard with a deeper sentiment of gratitude than it had ever raised before. . .

Blessed is the one who finds wisdom,
and the one who gets understanding.
Proverbs 3:13

Minute by minute, Elizabeth is growing in wisdom and understanding. Understanding of who Mr. Darcy truly is, how respectable he is, how skillfully he manages his beautiful estate, is softening Elizabeth's opinion of him. But the tinge of regret that she feels for refusing his proposal is tempered by the memory of his scorn concerning her family, even her aunt and uncle. Although her honest heart, and an absence from Mr. Darcy, are increasing Elizabeth's fondness for him, her wisdom guards her heart. Her acceptance of Mr. Darcy's proposal would have separated her from the family she loves. Mature and tender love does not require such a sacrifice.

DAY NINETY-THREE

෴

As they walked across the lawn towards the river, Elizabeth turned back to look again; her uncle and aunt stopped also, and while the former was conjecturing as to the date of the building, the owner of it himself suddenly came forward from the road. . .

They were within twenty yards of each other, and so abrupt was his appearance that it was impossible to avoid his sight. Their eyes instantly met, and the cheeks of each were overspread with the deepest blush. He absolutely started, and for a moment seemed immovable from surprise; but shortly recovering himself, advanced towards the party, and spoke to Elizabeth, if not in terms of perfect composure, at least of perfect civility.

She had instinctively turned away; but stopping on his approach, received his compliments with an embarrassment impossible to be overcome.

. . . She blushed again and again over the perverseness of the meeting. And his behavior. . .what could it mean? That he should even speak to her was amazing. . . What a contrast did it offer to his last address in Rosings park, when he put his letter into her hand! She knew not what to think, or how to account for it.

Her astonishment. . .was extreme, and continually was she repeating, "Why is he so altered? From what can it proceed? It cannot be for me. . . My reproofs at Hunsford could not work such a change as this. It is impossible that he should still love me."

Love never ends.
I Corinthians 13:8

※

Elizabeth's chance encounter with Mr. Darcy while touring his home caused her to blush deeply for the rest of the day, but Mr. Darcy's civil behavior towards her and her family made her think. Does he still love her despite the vehemence with which she rejected his offer of marriage back in Hunsford? That he would tenderly ask about her family, converse openly with her aunt and uncle, and desire to introduce his sister to her, all pointed to a continued affection. True love is enduring; it sees past angry words and hurts and loves faithfully. This truth has Elizabeth in awe.

DAY NINETY-FOUR

※

Elizabeth had settled it that Mr. Darcy would bring his sister to visit her the very day after her reaching Pemberley. . .

Since her being at Lambton, she had heard that Miss Darcy was exceedingly proud; but the observation of a very few minutes convinced her that she was only exceedingly shy.

They had not been long together before Darcy told her that Bingley was also coming to wait on her. . . All Elizabeth's anger against him had been long done away; but had she still felt any, it could hardly have stood its ground against the unaffected cordiality with which he expressed himself on seeing her again.

. . . It was not often that she could turn her eyes on Mr. Darcy himself; but, whenever she did catch a glimpse, she saw an expression of general complaisance. . .and courting the good opinion of people with whom any intercourse a few months ago would have been a disgrace. . .

Eager to be alone, and fearful of inquiries or hints from her uncle and aunt. . .she hurried away to dress.

But she had no reason to fear Mr. and Mrs. Gardiner's curiosity. . . It was evident that she was much better acquainted with Mr. Darcy than they had before any idea of it; it was evident that he was very much in love with her.

. . . love is strong as death. . .
Song of Solomon 8:6

❧

As strong as death is to eternally separate, enduring love is stronger. Love can mend and join for eternity. Mr. Darcy's solid love for Elizabeth is evident as he introduces his sister, gets to know her family, and re-admits Bingley to the group. Mr. Darcy's former pride has melted away: dissolved by his ardent love for Elizabeth, and a desire that she know how willing he is to improve his weaknesses to win her. Mr. Darcy's love is stronger than death: seeking to heal the wounds that were caused by his pride.

DAY NINETY-FIVE

⁂

Convinced as Elizabeth now was that Miss Bingley's dislike of her had originated in jealousy, she could not help feeling how very unwelcome her appearance at Pemberley must be to her, and was curious to know with how much civility on that lady's side the acquaintance would now be renewed...

"Pray, Miss Eliza, are not the militia removed from Meryton? They must be a great loss to *your* family..."

Had Miss Bingley known what pain she was then giving her beloved friend, she undoubtedly would have refrained from the hint; but she had nearly intended to discompose Elizabeth.

...and while Mr. Darcy was attending them to their carriage, Miss Bingley was venting her feelings in criticisms on Elizabeth's person, behavior, and dress. But Georgiana would not join her. Her brother's recommendation was enough to ensure her favor...

"How very ill Eliza Bennet looks this morning, Mr. Darcy," she cried; "...I must confess that I never could see any beauty in her..."

Persuaded as Miss Bingley was that Darcy admired Elizabeth, this was not the best method of recommending herself; but angry people are not always wise...

"I particularly recollect your saying one night... '*She* a beauty! I should as soon call her mother a wit...'"

"Yes," replied Darcy, who could contain himself no longer, "but *that* was only when I first knew her, for it is many months since I have considered her as one of the handsomest women of my acquaintance."

*A man without self-control
is like a city broken into and left without walls.*
Proverbs 25:28

The visit to Pemberley affected various results. Mrs. Gardiner became more convinced of Mr. Darcy's regard for Elizabeth and longed to engage her niece in talking about him. Elizabeth became more convinced of Georgiana's painful shyness and Darcy's eagerness to see them get to know one another better. Caroline Bingley, on the other hand, was convinced of Mr. Darcy's partiality for Elizabeth. Caroline allowed her jealousy and anger to attempt to belittle Elizabeth in front of Darcy. This unwise approach merely backfired: Darcy let her know how much he cared for Elizabeth by complimenting her beauty. Caroline's desperation has brought her to a place of vulnerability. Her jealousy is exposing her spirit to pain, like an unwalled city is exposed to attack. By practicing control, she would have at least protected herself from creating her own broken heart.

❧❧

"Oh! where, is my uncle?" cired Elizabeth, darting from her seat as she finished the letter. . .but as she reached the door it was opened by a servant and Mr. Darcy appeared. . .

"Good God! what is the matter?" cried he, with more feeling than politeness. . .

"There is nothing the matter with me. . . I am only distressed by some dreadful news which I have just received from Longbourn. . . My youngest sister has left all her friends--has eloped; has thrown herself into the power of--of Mr. Wickham. . . I might have prevented it! Had his character been known, this could not have happened. . ."

Darcy made no answer. He seemed scarcely to hear her, and was walking up and down the room in earnest meditation. . . Elizabeth soon observed and instantly understood it. . .and never had she so honestly felt that she could have loved him, as now, when all love must be vain. . .

As he quitted the room, Elizabeth felt how improbable it was that they should ever see each other again on such terms of cordiality as had marked their several meetings in Derbyshire. . .

Love one another with brotherly affection.
Outdo one another in showing honor.
Romans 12:10

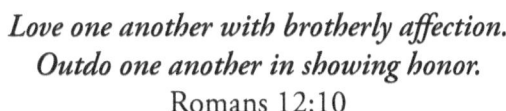

Although Mr. Darcy's kind affection for Elizabeth has become obvious, Lydia's actions have tainted the whole family. Elizabeth's gratitude for Mr. Darcy's discretion and esteem for his strong character causes her to honor him in her heart. Now that all hope for a future relationship has been dashed by the family's shame, Elizabeth realizes that she loves Mr. Darcy. This love started with respect and grew into a strong desire to see him do well and a desire to be a part of that for him. Sadly, humanity often does not realize what it possesses until it has been taken away. With heaviness of heart, Elizabeth and her aunt and uncle begin the journey back to Longbourn. Regret lay behind and trouble lay ahead.

DAY NINETY-SEVEN

❧❧

"I have been thinking it over again, Elizabeth," said her uncle, as they drove from the town. . . "It appears to me so very unlikely that any young man should form such a design against a girl who is by no means unprotected or friendless. . . His temptation is not adequate to the risk!"

. . . "Upon my word," said Mrs. Gardiner, "I begin to be of your uncle's opinion. It is really too great a violation of decency, honor and interest for him to be guilty of it. . ."

"But why all this secrecy. . . Why must their marriage be private? Oh, no--this is not likely. . . Wickham will never marry a woman without some money. . ."

"But can you think that Lydia is so lost to everything but love of him as to consent to live with him on any other terms than marriage?"

"It does seem, and it is most shocking indeed," replied Elizabeth, with tears in her eyes, that a sister's sense of decency and virtue in such a point should admit of doubt. But really, I know not what to say. . .she has never been taught to think on serious subjects; and for the last half--nay, for a twelve-month--she has been given up to nothing but amusement and vanity. . . And we all know that Wickham has every charm of person and address that can captivate a woman. . . But Jane knows as well as I do what Wickham really is. We both know that he has been profligate in every sense of the word; that he has neither integrity nor honor; that he is as false and deceitful as he is insinuating."

Whoever walks in integrity will be delivered,
but he who is crooked in his ways
will suddenly fall.
Romans 12:10

Elizabeth regrets her decision to not expose the true Wickham. By grasping the easier thing to do, and by allowing Lydia's foolish vanity to be touched by George Wickham's deceitful and insinuating character, Elizabeth felt all the weight of what had occurred. But her evidence of his maliciousness, as it concerned preying on young women, was guarded by the secrecy she promised Darcy when he told of the situation with Georgiana. The Gardiners did not believe that Wickham would have deliberately singled out Lydia as an object of love, if he truly knew how poor she was. But Wickham's past choices and poor character convinced Elizabeth that he was capable of any degradation, including seducing a poor and foolish young woman for his own benefit.

DAY NINETY-EIGHT

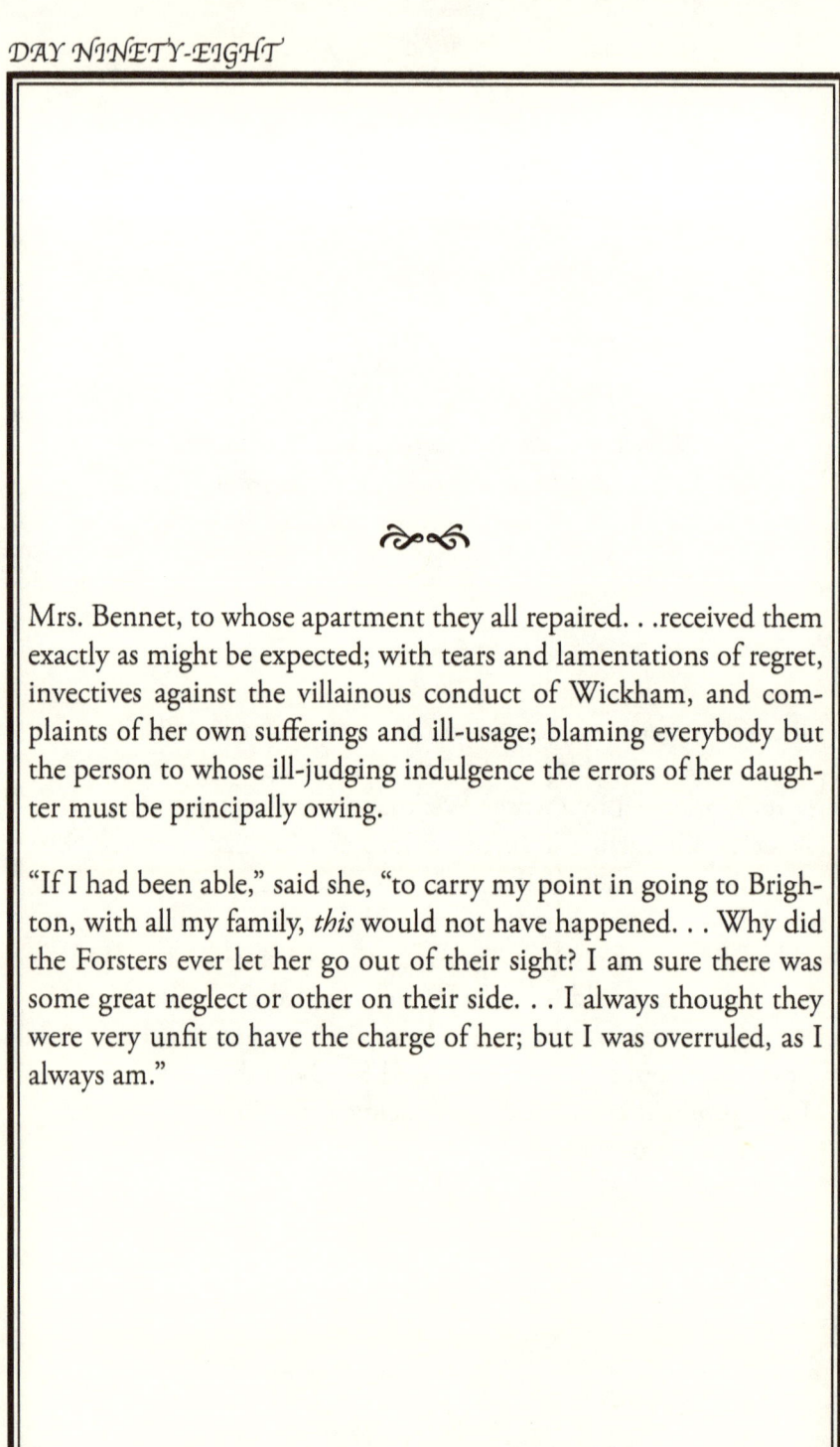

Mrs. Bennet, to whose apartment they all repaired. . .received them exactly as might be expected; with tears and lamentations of regret, invectives against the villainous conduct of Wickham, and complaints of her own sufferings and ill-usage; blaming everybody but the person to whose ill-judging indulgence the errors of her daughter must be principally owing.

"If I had been able," said she, "to carry my point in going to Brighton, with all my family, *this* would not have happened. . . Why did the Forsters ever let her go out of their sight? I am sure there was some great neglect or other on their side. . . I always thought they were very unfit to have the charge of her; but I was overruled, as I always am."

The wisest of women builds her house,
but folly with her own hands tears it down.
Proverbs 14:1

Mrs. Bennet, whose foolish, selfish living, has created Lydia, either by commission or omission, blames everyone else for the current situation. She places blame on Wickham's evil character, blame on Mr. Bennet for not taking the whole family to Brighton, and blame on the Fosters for not protecting Lydia better. Her inability to see her role in the raising of a foolish, self-centered daughter, merely exposes the depths of her lack of maturity and wisdom. Lydia obtained her ignorance, selfishness, and foolishness from the example and indulgence of her own mother. Regret and not blame, should be pouring from the lips of Mrs. Bennet!

DAY NINETY-NINE

⁓⁓

"Kitty then owned, with a very natural triumph on knowing more than the rest of us, that Lydia's last letter, she had prepared her for such a step. She had known, it seems, of their being in love with each other many weeks."

. . . " Could Colonel Forster repeat the particulars of Lydia's note to his wife?"

"He brought it with him for us to see."

Jane then took it from her pocketbook and gave it to Elizabeth.

These were its contents:

"MY DEAR HARRIET,
"You will laugh when you know where I am gone. . . I am going to Gretna Green, and if you cannot guess with who, I shall think you a simpleton, for there is but one man in the world I love, and he is an angel. . . You need not send them word at Longbourn of my going, if you do not like it, for it will make the surprise the greater, when I write to them and sign my name 'Lydia Wickham.' What a good joke it will be! I can hardly write for laughing. . . Your affectionate friend,

"LYDIA BENNET."

"Oh! thoughtless, thoughtless Lydia!" cried Elizabeth. . . "What a letter to be written at such a moment!"

The woman Folly is loud;
she is seductive and knows nothing.
Proverbs 9:13

☙◈❧

The extent of Lydia's foolishness and simple-minded selfishness was exposed by her letter. While her family and friends are bemoaning her poor choice, she treats the subject of elopement with mocking and laughter. The financial imprudence of the match never occurred to her. That Wickham was as poor as herself never gave a moment's hesitation. In Proverbs chapter one, Wisdom cries out to the foolish to forsake their foolishness and grasp knowledge and understanding. Lydia's deliberate choice to be simple-minded, encouraged by her foolish mother, can only lead her down a path of misery, and leave her family to suffer the repercussions.

DAY ONE HUNDRED

‏❧

The whole party were in hopes of a letter from Mr. Bennet. . .but the post came in without bringing a single line from him. . . Mr. Gardiner had waited only for the letters before he set off. . .

As Mrs. Gardiner began to wish to be at home, it was settled that she and her children should go to London, at the same time that Mr. Bennet came from it. . .

When Mr. Bennet arrived, he had all the appearance of his usual philosophic composure. He said as little as he had ever been in the habit of saying. . .and it was some time before his daughters had courage to speak of it.

. . . Elizabeth ventured to introduce the subject; and then, on her briefly expressing her sorrow for what he must have endured, he replied, "Say nothing of that. Who should suffer but myself? It has been my own doing, and I ought to feel it."

"You must not be too severe upon yourself," replied Elizabeth.

"You may well warn me against such an evil. . . No, Lizzy, let me once in my life feel how much I have been to blame. I am not afraid of being overpowered by the impression. It will pass away soon enough. . . Lizzy, I bear you no ill will for being justified in your advice to me last May, which, considering the event, shows some greatness of mind."

*A foolish son is a grief to his father
and bitterness to her who bore him.*
Proverbs 17:25

❧

This verse implies that the child was taught to be wise by wise parents but rejected their teachings. Mr. Bennet feels all the weight of the truth of the verse, but confesses his shame concerning his hands-off approach to parenting. By taking the easy way, by pleasing himself for years and retreating to his library to read in peace, Mr. Bennet, by neglect, has raised a foolish child in Lydia. Mr. Bennet has proved that non-parenting can have just as negative of a result as bad parenting. Another scripture suggests that "a child left to himself brings his parents shame." Every human is in need of skilled guidance from an older and wiser person, and Lydia displays this truth perfectly.

DAY ONE HUNDRED AND ONE

᚛᚜

"MY DEAR BROTHER:

"At last I am able to send you some tidings of my niece, and such as, upon the whole, will give you satisfaction... It is enough to know they are discovered. I have seen them both. They are not married, nor can I find there any intention of being so; but if you are willing to perform the engagements which I have ventured to make on your side, I hope it will not be long before they are. All that is required of you is, to assure to your daughter by settlement, her equal share of the five thousand pounds secured among your children after the decease of yourself and my sister; and, moreover, to enter into an engagement of allowing her, during your life, one hundred pounds per annum... You will easily comprehend, from these particulars, that Mr. Wickham's circumstances are not so hopeless as they are generally believed to be. The world has been deceived in the respect; and I am happy to say there will be some little money, even when all his debts are discharged, to settle on my niece...stay quietly at Longbourn...we have judged it best that my niece should be married from this house... Yours, etc.

"EDW. GARDINER."

... "Yes, yes, they must marry. There is nothing else to be done. But there are two things that I want very much to know--one is, how much money your uncle has laid down to bring it about; and the other, how I am ever to pay him."

An excellent wife who can find?
She is far more precious than jewels.
Proverbs 31:10

❦

Lydia Bennet's value as a foolish woman is so low, that it seems obvious that Mr. Gardiner had to put out an immense sum of money to convince Wickham to marry her. Since they were discovered living together, with no intention of marrying, Lydia's value as a virtuous woman was nothing. May we always be mindful of this fact: our true worth is first, being created in the image of God, and second, being redeemed by the sacrifice of His Son. Who we are and whose we are!

DAY ONE HUNDRED AND TWO

✤

Elizabeth was now most heartily sorry that she had, from the distress of the moment, been led to make Mr. Darcy acquainted with their fears for her sister; for since her marriage would so shortly give the proper termination to the elopement, they might hope to conceal its unfavorable beginning from all those who were not immediately on the spot. . . Had Lydia's marriage been concluded on the most honorable terms, it was not to be supposed that Mr. Darcy would connect himself with a family where, to every other objection, would now be added an alliance and relationship of the nearest kind with the man whom he so justly scorned. . .

She was humbled, she was grieved; she repented, though she hardly knew of what. . . She was convinced that she could have been happy with him when it was no longer likely they would meet. . .

She began now to comprehend that he was exactly the man who . . .would most suit her. It was a union that must have been to the advantage of both: by her ease and liveliness, his mind might have been softened, his manners improved; and from his judgment, information, and knowledge of the world, she must have received benefit of greater importance.

*The plans of the heart belong to man,
but the answer of the tongue is from the Lord.*
Proverbs 16:1

In the midst of the chaos and clamor of her home, Elizabeth found quiet moments to reflect on her obvious change of heart concerning Mr. Darcy. Now when she was fully aware that all chance was lost, she recognized that he was exactly the man that would meld with her personality. She understood how she could enhance him; and she admitted how much he could influence her with his strong mind and character. In fact, it is the LORD that prepares hearts, personalities, and circumstances in order to join them together in friendship or love. Is there such a thing as "the one?" That is not certain, but it is certain that God is in the business of preparing souls to perfectly complement one another.

DAY ONE HUNDRED AND THREE

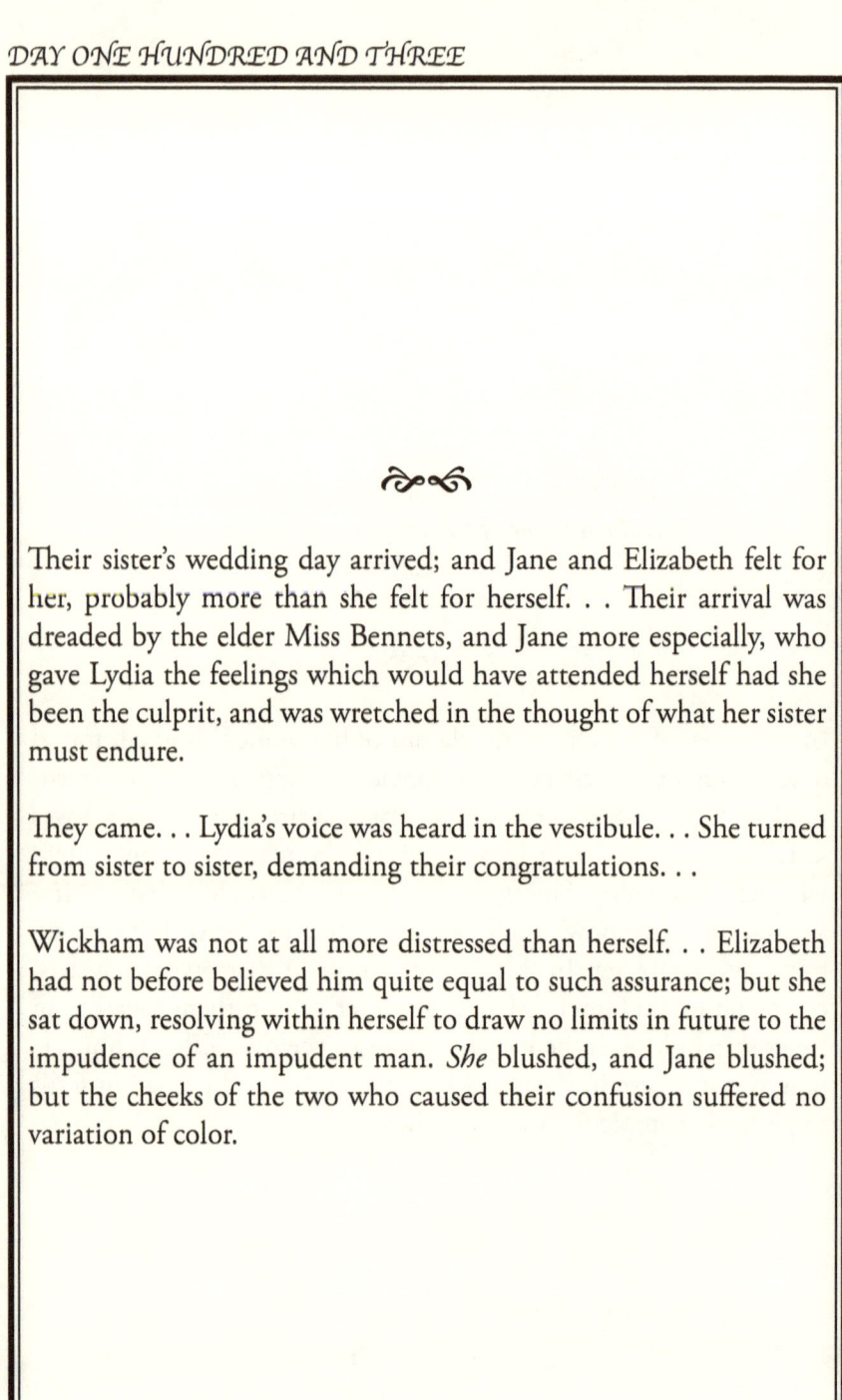

Their sister's wedding day arrived; and Jane and Elizabeth felt for her, probably more than she felt for herself. . . Their arrival was dreaded by the elder Miss Bennets, and Jane more especially, who gave Lydia the feelings which would have attended herself had she been the culprit, and was wretched in the thought of what her sister must endure.

They came. . . Lydia's voice was heard in the vestibule. . . She turned from sister to sister, demanding their congratulations. . .

Wickham was not at all more distressed than herself. . . Elizabeth had not before believed him quite equal to such assurance; but she sat down, resolving within herself to draw no limits in future to the impudence of an impudent man. *She* blushed, and Jane blushed; but the cheeks of the two who caused their confusion suffered no variation of color.

*This is the way of an adulteress:
she eats and wipes her mouth
and says, 'I have done no wrong.'*
Proverbs 30:20

Elizabeth and Jane are feeling all the shame and embarrassment that Lydia should have been feeling. After living with Wickham for weeks with no intention of marrying, after causing anguish to her family, after being forced to marry to preserve the family's honor, Lydia walks back into her home as if she is a queen. Without blushing over her behavior, she demanded congratulations on her marriage to Wickham. There is nothing more shameful than a person allowing others to feel her dishonor and not feeling the weight of it herself.

DAY ONE HUNDRED AND FOUR

Elizabeth had the satisfaction of receiving an answer to her letter as soon as she possibly could. . .

"MY DEAR NIECE,
"I have just received your letter, and shall devote this whole morning to answering it. . . On the very day of my coming home from Longbourn, your uncle had a most unexpected visitor. Mr. Darcy called, and was shut up with several hours. . . He came to tell Mr. Gardiner that he had found out where your sister and Mr. Wickham were. . .and came to town with the resolution of hunting for them. . . He saw Wickham and afterwards insisted on seeing Lydia. His first object with her, he acknowledged, had been to persuade her to quit her present disgraceful situation. . . offering his assistance as far as it would go. But he found Lydia absolutely resolved on remaining where she was. . . Since such were her feelings, it only remained, he thought, to secure and expedite, which, in his very first conversation with Wickham, he easily learned had never been *his* design. . . Mr. Darcy asked him why he had not married your sister at once. . .he found, in reply to this question, that Wickham still cherished the hope of more effectually making his fortune by marriage in some other country. Under such circumstances, however, he was not likely to be proof against the temptation of immediate relief. They met several times, for there was much to be discussed. Wickham, of course, wanted more than he could get, but at length, was reduced to be reasonable. Everything being settled between *them,* Mr. Darcy's next step was to make your uncle acquainted with it. . . "Yours, very sincerely,

"M. GARDINER."

The contents of this letter threw Elizabeth into a flutter of spirits, in which it was difficult to determine whether pleasure or pain bore the greatest share.

A friend loves at all times...
Proverbs 17:17

That Mr. Darcy's motives in fixing the situation concerning Lydia is motivated by his love for Elizabeth, seemed obvious to the Gardiners. Their agreeing to the arrangement of letting Darcy carry all the financial burden, was due to the firm conviction that there was a solid relationship between Mr. Darcy and their niece. Elizabeth's confession of surprise merely confirmed their conviction that love alone was Mr. Darcy's motive in humbling himself concerning Wickham, Lydia, and his potential future with the Bennet family. Darcy is the picture of faithful, humble, sacrificial love. And Elizabeth was not sure what to think.

[Elizabeth] was roused from her seat and her reflections by someone's approach; and before she could strike another path, she was overtaken by Wickham.

"I am afraid I interrupt your solitary ramble, my dear sister?" said he, as he joined her.

"You certainly do," she replied with a smile; "but it does not follow that the interruption must be unwelcome."

"I should be sorry indeed if it were. . . I find from our uncle and aunt that you have actually seen Pemberley . . . And you saw the old housekeeper, I suppose? Poor Reynolds, she was always very fond of me. But of course she did not mention my name to you."

"Yes, she did."

"And what did she say?"

"That you were gone into the army, and, she was afraid, had--not turned out well. At such a distance as *that*, you know that things are strangely misrepresented. . ."

"I was surprised to see Darcy in town last month. . . Did you see him while you were at Lambton? I thought I understood from the Gardiners that you had."

"Yes; he introduced us to his sister."

"Did you go by the village of Kympton? . . . I mention it because it is the living which I ought to have had. . . It would have suited me in every respect. . ."

"I have heard, from authority, which I thought as good, that it was left to you conditionally only, and at the will of the present patron. . . I did hear, too, that there was a time when sermon making was not so palatable to you as it seems to be at present--that you actually declared your resolution of never taking orders, and that the business had been compromised accordingly."

They were now almost at the door of the house. . .and, unwilling for her sister's sake, to provoke him, she only said. . . "Come, Mr. Wickham, we are brother and sister, you know. Do not let us quarrel about the past. In future, I hope we shall be always of one mind."

She held out her hand; he kissed it with affectionate gallantry, though he hardly knew how to look, and they entered the house.

*The wicked flee when no one pursues,
but the righteous are bold as a lion.*
Proverbs 28:1

Elizabeth, bold in her solid knowledge of who Mr. Wickham truly was, began a game of cat and mouse with him. From several reliable sources, she had learned that all he had originally told her about his past was a lie. From his present behavior with Lydia, and all that needed to happen to patch up their reputations, Elizabeth was confident. She knew George Wickham, the real one. This knowledge gave her courage and weakened him. As the conversation touched on his past sins, he grew increasingly uncomfortable, while Elizabeth grew in assurance. Jesus declared that the truth can set people free. In this case, Elizabeth was free to understand much: who she was, who George Wickham was, and who Mr. Darcy truly was. This was the truth that had set her free from the lies of her own pride and prejudice.

DAY ONE HUNDRED AND SIX

❧

"Well, well, and so Mr. Bingley is coming down, sister," (for Mrs. Philips first brought the news).

Miss Bennet had not been able to hear of his coming without changing color.

"I saw you look at me today, Lizzy, when my aunt told us of the present report; and I know I appeared distressed; but don't imagine it was from any silly cause. I was only confused for a moment. . . I do assure you that the news does not affect me either with pleasure or pain. . . I dread other people's remarks."

Elizabeth did not know what to make of it. . .

In spite of what her sister declared. . .in the expectation of his arrival, Elizabeth could easily perceive that her spirits were affected by it. They were more disturbed, more unequal, then she had often seen them. . .

"I begin to be sorry that he comes at all," said Jane to her sister. "It would be nothing. . .but I can hardly bear to hear it thus perpetually talked of. My mother means well; but she does not know--no one can know--how much I suffer from what she says. Happy shall I be when his stay at Netherfield is over!"

*There is one whose rash words are like
sword thrusts,
but the tongue of the wise brings healing.*
Proverbs 12:18

☙❧

Mrs. Bennet's foolish, incessant ramblings concerning Mr. Bingley and his purpose for returning to the neighborhood are painful for Jane. Jane hardly knows her own feelings on the subject and is confused by her own ruffled spirits. Elizabeth feels her sister's hurt.

But Mrs. Bennet, who is only capable of thinking of herself, continues to pierce her own daughter's soul with her speculations. Speaking healthful and wise words is a gift that can be honed for the benefit of our listeners.

DAY ONE HUNDRED AND SEVEN

※

Mr. Bingley arrived. . . Elizabeth, to satisfy her mother, went to the window. . .she saw Mr. Darcy with him. . .

"Good gracious! Mr. Darcy! . . .Well, any friend of Mr. Bingley's will always be welcome here, to be sure; but else I must say that I hate the very sight of him."

Jane looked at Elizabeth with surprise and concern. She knew but little of their meeting in Derbyshire, and therefore felt for the awkwardness which must attend her sister. . . Each felt for the other . . . and their mother talked on, of her dislike of Mr. Darcy, and her resolution to be civil to him only as Mr. Bingley's friend. . . But Elizabeth had sources of uneasiness which could not be suspected by Jane. . . He was the person to whom the whole family were indebted.

. . . On the gentlemen's appearing. . . She had ventured only one glance at Darcy. He looked serious as usual, and, more. . .as she had seen him at Pemberley. But, perhaps, he could not in her mother's presence be what he was with her uncle and aunt.

*But love your enemies, and do good, and lend,
expecting nothing in return, and your reward will
be great, and you will be sons of the Most High, for
he is kind to the ungrateful and the evil.*
Luke 6:35

❧❦

Although it is a stretch to compare Mr. Darcy to God, they share similar characteristics: namely humility and patience in the face of ingratitude. Mrs. Bennet owes the restoration of Lydia's reputation to Mr. Darcy. Although she is unaware of his involvement in Lydia's situation, Mrs. Bennet's being predisposed to disliking Mr. Darcy, causes her to treat him with disdain. Elizabeth knowing the complete story, is humiliated by her mother's behavior. But Darcy remains calm in the face of such hostility, enduring the censure for the hopes of his friend Bingley and his enduring love for Elizabeth.

DAY ONE HUNDRED AND EIGHT

∂⇔∂

When they repaired to the dining room, Elizabeth eagerly watched to see whether Bingley would take the place. . .by her sister. . . On entering the room, he seemed to hesitate; but Jane happened to look around, and happened to smile; it was decided--he placed himself by her. . .

His behavior to her sister was such, during dinner time, as showed and admiration of her which, though more guarded than formerly, persuaded Elizabeth, that if left wholly to himself, Jane's happiness, and his own, would be speedily secured. . .

"It has been a very agreeable day," said Miss Bennet to Elizabeth. . .

Elizabeth smiled.

"Lizzy, you must not do so. You must not suspect me. It mortifies me. I assure you that I have now learned to enjoy his conversation as an agreeable and sensible young man, without having a wish beyond it. . ."

"You are very cruel," said her sister; "you will not let me smile, and are provoking me to it every moment."

"How hard it is in some cases to be believed! . . . But why should you wish to persuade me that I feel more than I acknowledge?"

Every way of a man is right in his own eyes,
but the Lord weighs the heart.
Proverbs 21:2

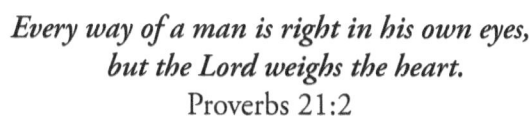

Jane is positive that her heart is no longer vulnerable to falling in love with Mr. Bingley, but Elizabeth is not convinced. After an evening of observing Bingley in Jane's presence, she realizes that Jane is causing his feelings to be renewed. But Jane is solid in her claims of being indifferent, of merely enjoying his company. Proverbs boldly states that humans are not very good at discerning their own thoughts, that only God Himself sees our true motives and intentions. Here Elizabeth sees more of Jane's mind than she does herself. Jane is merely trying to talk herself out of love to protect her heart from being wounded a second time.

DAY ONE HUNDRED AND NINE

༄༅

Jane could have no reserves from Elizabeth, where confidence would give pleasure; and instantly embracing her, acknowledged with the liveliest emotion, that she was the happiest creature in the world. "'Tis too much," she added,-- "By far too much. I do not deserve it. Oh! why is not everybody as happy!"

Elizabeth's congratulations were given with a sincerity, a warmth, a delight, which words could but poorly express. Every sentence of kindness was a fresh source of happiness to Jane.

Hope deferred makes the heart sick,
but a desire fulfilled is a tree of life.
Proverbs 13:12

☙❧

After almost a year of managing her broken heart, Jane's hope has been fulfilled by the proposal of Charles Bingley. Her happiness now exceeds the sorrow of the past, and she shares her joy with her family. Hopes in life are often interrupted or delayed, sometimes by circumstances and sometimes by the interferences of people. The Scripture encourages man to place his ultimate hope in God Himself, Who never disappoints. God is able to change the hopelessness of life into a completed dream, that gives joy to many. When life seems dreary and bleak, place hope in the Hope Giver, God.

DAY ONE HUNDRED AND TEN

∽✦∽

"You can be at no loss, Miss Bennet, to understand the reason of my journey hither. . . A report of a most alarming nature reached me two days ago. . . That you, that Miss Elizabeth Bennet, would, in all likelihood be united to my nephew--my own nephew--Mr. Darcy. Though I *know* it must be a scandalous falsehood. . . I instantly resolved on setting off for this place, that I might make my sentiments known to you."

"If you believed it impossible to be true," said Elizabeth. . . "I wonder you took the trouble of coming so far. . . Your coming to Longbourn, to see me and my family. . .will be rather a confirmation of it; if, indeed, such a report is in existence."

"If! do you, then, pretend to be ignorant of it? . . . Do you not know that such a report is spread abroad?"

"I never heard that it was."

. . . "Let me be rightly understood. . . Mr. Darcy is engaged to *my daughter*. . . From their infancy, they have been intended for eachother. . . Are you lost to every feeling of propriety and delicacy?"

". . . If Mr. Darcy is neither by honor nor inclination confined to his cousin, why is not he to make another choice? and if I am that choice, why may I not accept him?"

"Because honor, decorum, prudence--nay, interest, forbid it. . . You will be censured, slighted, and despised by everyone connected with him."

"These are heavy misfortunes," replied Elizabeth. "But the wife of Mr. Darcy must have such extraordinary sources of happiness necessarily attached to her situation, that she could. . .have no cause to repine."

*'Scoffer' is the name of the arrogant, haughty man
who acts with arrogant pride.*
Proverbs 21:24

☙❧

Based upon a rumor, which Elizabeth herself has not yet heard, Lady Catherine makes the journey to Longbourn to determine if Elizabeth is truly engaged to Mr. Darcy, her nephew. By her haughty attitude and condescending manners, Lady Catherine sought to insult Elizabeth enough to get her to deny the rumor, but the rampage has the opposite effect. Elizabeth is fully aware that Lady Catherine's demands have nothing to do with her own happiness. She denies having heard of such a report, but she refuses to promise never to become engaged to Mr. Darcy. Elizabeth is determined that her visitor's pride will not affect the happiness of her own future. True happiness is internal, and Elizabeth is aware that her allegiance is to Mr. Darcy and herself, and not to his scornful relatives. Her allegiance should form the basis for her decisions and responses.

DAY ONE HUNDRED AND ELEVEN

❧☙

The next morning, as she was going downstairs, she was met by her father. . .with a letter in his hand.

. . . "I have received a letter this morning that has astonished me exceedingly. As it principally concerns yourself, you ought to know its contents. I did not know before that I had *two* daughters on the brink of matrimony. Let me congratulate you on a very important conquest."

The color now rushed into Elizabeth's cheeks in the instantaneous conviction of its being a letter from the nephew, instead of the aunt . . .when her father continued. . .

"This letter is from Mr. Collins. . . He begins with congratulations on the approaching nuptials of my eldest daughter. . . What relates to yourself is as follows: 'Your daughter Elizabeth, it is presumed, will not long bear the name of Bennet. . .and the chosen partner of her fate may be reasonably looked up to as one of the most illustrious personages in this land. . . My motive for cautioning you is as follows. We have reason to imagine that his aunt, Lady Catherine de Bourgh, does not look on this match with a friendly eye.' Mr. Darcy, you see, is the man! . . . Mr. Darcy, who never looks at any woman but to see a blemish, and who probably never looked at *you* in his life? It is admirable! . . . Had they fixed on any other man, it would have been nothing; but *his* perfect indifference, and *your* pointed dislike, make it so delightfully absurd!"

*Like cold water to a thirsty soul,
so is good news from a far country.*
Proverbs 25:25

What gave her father great entertainment, Elizabeth found alarming! What could be the origins of the rumor of Mr. Darcy soon being engaged to her? Who was this good authority? Although the letter should have brought her joy and hope, it merely made the way seem foggy and unclear.

First Lady Catherine coming to frighten her out of a supposed engagement, then a letter from Mr. Collins with both a congratulations and a warning: what could it all mean? Finally, Elizabeth was disturbed by her father's amusement. Her vocal disdain of Mr. Darcy had tainted her whole family. Now that her feelings were quite the opposite, how could she listen to the objections of others? Objections mostly formed by her own outspoken prejudices.

Day One Hundred and Twelve

※

"Mr. Darcy, I am a very selfish creature; and for the sake of giving relief to my own feelings, care not how much I may be wounding yours. I can no longer help thanking you for your unexampled kindness to my poor sister. Ever since I have known it, I have been most anxious to acknowledge to you how gratefully I feel it. Were it known to the rest of my family, I should not have merely my own gratitude to express. . . Lydia's thoughtlessness first betrayed to me that you had been concerned in the matter and, of course, I could not rest till I knew the particulars. Let me thank you again and again . . .for that generous compassion which induced you to take so much trouble. . . for the sake of discovering them."

"If you *will* thank me," he replied, "let it be for yourself alone. . . Your *family* owe me nothing. Much as I respect them, I believe I thought only of *you*. . . You are too generous to trifle with me. If your feelings are still what they were last April, tell so at once. *My* affections and wishes are unchanged; but one word from you will silence me on this subject forever."

Elizabeth, feeling all the more than common awkwardness and anxiety of his situation, now forced herself to speak. . . Her sentiments had undergone so material a change. . .as to make her receive with gratitude and pleasure his present assurances. The happiness which this reply produced was such as he had probably never felt before, and he expressed himself on the occasion as sensibly and as warmly as a man violently in love can be supposed to do.

Love bears all things, believes all things, hopes all things, endures all things.
I Corinthians 13:7

Gratitude is said to have a powerful influence on love. Elizabeth, upon expressing her gratitude for all Mr. Darcy did for her sister, Lydia, opened the gate for Mr. Darcy to express once again how much he loved her. Elizabeth's thankfulness was the opening that Mr. Darcy was searching for to renew his proposal of the spring. Over the last half a year, Elizabeth's feelings concerning Mr. Darcy had altered slowly and completely. Where she once disdained him, she now felt only love, respect, and appreciation. Her positive response to this second appeal from Mr. Darcy for her heart was received with great joy. Mr. Darcy's love was enduring, despite Elizabeth's original rejection, and now bore fruit in a mutual, reciprocal love. Loves never fails.

DAY ONE HUNDRED AND THIRTEEN

☙❧

"It taught me to hope," said he, "as I had scarcely ever allowed myself to hope before. I knew enough of your disposition to be certain, that had you been absolutely, irrevocably decided against me, you would have acknowledged it to Lady Catherine, frankly and openly."

Elizabeth colored and laughed as she replied, "Yes, you know enough of my *frankness* to believe me capable of *that*. After abusing you so abominably to your face, I could have no scruple in abusing you to all your relations."

But let none of you suffer as a murderer or a thief
or an evildoer or as a meddler.
I Peter 4:15

Poor Lady Catherine! Her extreme pride and haughty manners caused her to assume that she had the right to interfere in the relationship between Darcy and Elizabeth. She had derided and belittled Elizabeth to her face in an attempt to prevent a rumored marriage to her nephew, Mr. Darcy. When that failed, Lady Catherine drove to London to meet Darcy and threaten him with Elizabeth's responses. Her hopes of turning Darcy against Elizabeth completely backfired. Elizabeth's frank answers caused Darcy to hope that there was a chance that she had changed her mind concerning him. Rather than turn them against each other, Lady Catherine's interference brought about a quick understanding of regard between them and a settled engagement. Thank you, Lady Catherine, for being used by true love to bring Mr. Darcy and Elizabeth together!

DAY ONE HUNDRED AND FOURTEEN

❧❦

"What did you say of me that I did not deserve? For, though your accusations were ill-founded, formed on mistaken premises, my behavior to you at the time had merited the severest reproof. It was unpardonable. I cannot think of it without abhorrence. . . The recollection of what I then said--of my conduct, my manners, my expressions during the whole of it--is now. . .inexpressibly painful to me. Your reproof, so well applied, I shall never forget: 'had you behaved in a more gentlemen like manner.' Those were your words. You know not, you can scarcely conceive, how they have tortured me;--though it was some time, I confess, before I was reasonable enough to allow their justice."

". . . I had not the smallest idea of their being ever felt in such a way."

. . . Darcy mentioned his letter. "Did it. . .soon make you think better of me?"

She explained what its effect on her had been, and how gradually all her former prejudices had been removed. . . "You must learn some of my philosophy. Think only of the past as its remembrance gives you pleasure."

. . . "What do I not owe you! You taught me a lesson; hard indeed, at first, but most advantageous. By you I was properly humbled. I came to you without a doubt of my reception. You showed me how insufficient were all my pretensions to please a woman worthy of being pleased."

"Had you then persuaded yourself that I should?"

"Indeed, I had. . . I believed you to be wishing, expecting my addresses."

". . . I never meant to intentionally deceive you, but my spirits might often lead me wrong. How you must have hated me after *that* evening!"

"Hate you! I was angry, perhaps, at first, but my anger soon began to take a proper direction."

☙❧

For by the grace given to me I say to everyone among you not to think of himself more highly than he ought to think, but to think with sober judgment, each according to the measure of faith that God has assigned.
Romans 12:3

☙❧

Mr. Darcy's humble confession concerning his life-long pride and conceit go a long way in permanently healing the rift between Elizabeth and himself. Although angry, at first, by the honesty of her accusations, Darcy slowly allowed her reproof to sink into his heart and spirit. By truthfully scrutinizing his attitude and manners in the light of Elizabeth's rejection, he came to understand himself better. He acknowledged that he had been allowed, even encouraged, by his parents to pursue good principles with a wrong spirit. Mr. Darcy's spontaneous gratitude for Elizabeth's honest words is a beautiful example of his fervent love for her. Honest, humble confession is not only good for the soul, but it is a beautiful way to begin a life-long relationship. Mr. Darcy, we love you!

DAY ONE HUNDRED AND FIFTEEN

∽∾

"I am almost afraid of asking what you thought of me when we met at Pemberley. You blamed me for coming?"

"No, indeed, I felt nothing but surprise. . . My object then. . .was to show you, by every civility in my power, that I was not so mean as to resent the past; I hoped to obtain your forgiveness, to lessen your ill opinion, by letting you see that your reproofs had been attended to."

. . . "What could have become of Mr. Bingley!" was a wonder which introduced the discussion of *their* affairs. . .

"On the evening before my going to London. . . I made a confession to him which I believe I ought to have made long ago. I told him of all that had occurred to make my former interference in his affairs absurd and impertinent. His surprise was great. I told him. . .that I believed myself mistaken in supposing. . .that your sister was indifferent to him; and. . .I felt no doubt of their happiness together. . . I had narrowly observed her during the two visits. . .and I was convinced of her affection. . . I was obliged to confess one thing that which. . . offended him. I could not allow myself to conceal that your sister had been in town for three months last winter. . . and purposefully kept it from him. He was angry. . .but. . .has heartily forgiven me now."

Elizabeth longed to observe that Mr. Bingley had been a most delightful friend--so easily guided. . .but she checked herself. She remembered that he had yet to learn to be laughed at, and it was rather too early to begin.

. . . and you will know the truth,
and the truth will set you free.
John 8:32

❧

By embracing the truth, Mr. Darcy was able to confess his weaknesses to himself, to Elizabeth, and to his friend, Charles Bingley. Elizabeth's reproofs at the time of his original proposal at first made him angry at her, but as he let them sink into his heart, he rightfully turned the anger against himself. He clearly saw the depths of his pride and arrogance. When he unexpectedly met Elizabeth at his home at Pemberley, his one goal was to convince her that he had changed because of the rebuke that she had given him. The last person who needed to hear his confession was his friend, Bingley. Darcy's confession that he interfered in his relationship with Jane, even lying by omission, made Bingley angry. Thankfully his friend's anger lasted only as long as it took to convince Jane of his continuing love. Speaking the truth to himself and others truly set Mr. Darcy free. Free to love Elizabeth and free to be an honest friend to Bingley.

At night she opened her heart to Jane. Though suspicion was very far from Miss Bennet's general habits, she was absolutely incredulous here.

"You are joking, Lizzy. This cannot be! engaged to Mr. Darcy! . . . I know it to be impossible."

". . . I am in earnest. I speak nothing but the truth. He still loves me, and we are engaged."

Jane looked at her doubtingly, "Oh, Lizzy! it cannot be. I know how much you dislike him."

"You know nothing of the matter. *That* is all to be forgot. Perhaps, I did not always love him so well as I do now. But in such cases as these a good memory is unpardonable. "

". . . My dear, dear, Lizzy. . . I do congratulate you--but are you certain. . .that you can be happy with him?"

"There can be no doubt of that. It is settled between us already that we are to be the happiest couple in the world. But are you pleased, Jane? Shall you like to have such a brother?"

"Very, very much. Nothing could give either Bingley or myself more delight. . . Let me know everything that I am to know, without delay. Will you tell me how long you have loved him?"

"It has been coming on so gradually, that I hardly know when it began. But I believe I must date it from my first seeing his beautiful grounds at Pemberley."

Another entreaty that she would be serious, however, produced the desired effect, and she soon satisfied Jane by her solemn assurances of attachment. When convinced on that article, Miss Bennet had nothing further to wish.

... complete my joy by being of the same mind,
having the same love,
being in full accord and of one mind.
Philippians 2:2

Elizabeth's attempt to share her joyful, good news concerning her engagement to Mr. Darcy, with her sister takes some effort. Elizabeth desires that Jane join her; agree with her on her happy new state. But her months of expressed prejudices about Darcy, and her rejection of his first proposal back in the spring, makes the task of convincing Jane of the truth very difficult, indeed. Elizabeth resorts to asking Jane to denounce her good memory, to forget the things that she had said about Darcy in the past. Once Jane truly believes that Elizabeth is being honest, she rejoices with her in her good news. Paul's admonition in Philippians 3:13 about forgetting the "things which are behind" is the same principle that helps Jane embrace Elizabeth, her engagement, and her future life of happiness.

DAY ONE HUNDRED AND SEVENTEEN

※

Her father was walking about the room, looking grave and anxious. "Lizzy," said he, "what are you doing? Are you out of your senses, to be accepting this man? Have you not always hated him?"

How earnestly did she then wish that her former opinions had been more reasonable, her expressions more moderate. . .and she assured him, with some confusion, of her deep attachment for Mr. Darcy . . . "Have you any other objection," said Elizabeth, "than your belief of my indifference?"

"None at all. We all know him to be a proud, unpleasant sort of man; but this would be nothing, if you really liked him."

"I do, I do like him," she replied, with tears in her eyes; "I love him. Indeed, he has no improper pride. He is perfectly amiable. You do not know what he really is. . .do not pain me by speaking of him in such terms."

"Lizzy," said her father, "I have given him my consent. He is the kind of man. . .I should never dare refuse anything which he condescended to ask. . . I know your disposition, Lizzy. I know that you could be neither happy nor respectable unless you truly esteemed your husband. . . My child, let me not have the grief of seeing *you* unable to respect your partner in life. . ."

Elizabeth. . .by repeated assurances. . .and enumerating with energy all his good qualities, she did conquer her father's incredulity, and reconcile him to the match.

To complete the favorable impression, she then told him what Mr. Darcy had voluntarily done for Lydia. He heard her with astonishment.

"This is an evening of wonders, indeed!"

Let all that you do be done in love.
I Corinthians 16:14

Because Elizabeth had so openly and vehemently spoken against Mr. Darcy during her days of prejudice, she had a difficult time convincing her father that she truly loved him. Mr. Bennet assumed that only Mr. Darcy's wealth was the attraction pulling Elizabeth toward an engagement with him. Elizabeth now regretted speaking her mind so freely.

With equal warmth, Elizabeth expressed her love and respect for Mr. Darcy, so moved that tears came to her eyes. Once her father was convinced of her depth of attachment, she revealed all that Darcy had done for their family by helping Lydia. Darcy's charity and depth of character made the difference. Mr. Bennet gave his hearty consent, "I could not have parted with you, my dear Lizzy, to anyone less worthy."

DAY ONE HUNDRED AND EIGHTEEN

&ஃ&

"Good gracious! Lord bless me! only think! dear me! Mr. Darcy. Who would have thought it. . . Oh, my sweetest Lizzy! how rich and how great you will be! What pin-money, what jewels, what carriages you will have! Jane's is nothing to it. . . Such a charming man!--so handsome! so tall! . . . A house in town! . . . Three daughters married! Ten thousand a year!"

This was enough to prove that her approbation need not be doubted; and Elizabeth, rejoicing that such an effusion was heard only by herself soon went away. But. . .her mother followed her.

"My dearest child. . .tell me what dish Mr. Darcy is particularly fond of that I may have it tomorrow."

This was a sad omen of what her mother's behavior to the gentleman himself might be. . . But the morrow past off much better than she expected; for Mrs. Bennet luckily stood in such awe of her intended son-in-law that she ventured not to speak to him, unless it was in her power to offer him any attention, or mark her deference for his opinion.

Elizabeth had the satisfaction of seeing her father taking pains to get acquainted with him; and Mr. Bennet soon assured her that he was rising every hour in his esteem.

For God shows no partiality.
Romans 2:11

*But if you show partiality, you are committing sin
and are convicted by the law as transgressors.*
James 2:9

☙❧

Mrs. Bennet, so simple-minded and changeable, soon begins to effuse praise of Elizabeth's engagement to a man that she had always despised. The attraction of his wealth and status creates the necessary "about-face" needed to praise Mr. Darcy, instead of disdain him, as Mrs. Bennet had done only the day before. Mr. Bennet had been assured by Elizabeth's love and by Darcy's character and generosity, but Mrs. Bennet, a respecter of persons, is convinced by the rise in esteem that Elizabeth and their family will undergo as a result of such a marriage union. May we always cleave to Mr. Bennet's wisdom, and always scorn Mrs. Bennet's folly: who a person is internally, is always more vital than how they are displayed externally. Character over possessions.

Elizabeth's spirits soon rose to playfulness again, she wanted Mr. Darcy to account for his having ever fallen in love with her. "How could you begin?" said she.

"I cannot fix on the hour, or the spot, or the look, or the words, which laid the foundation. . . I was already in the middle before I knew that I *had* begun."

". . . Now, be sincere; did you admire me for my impertinence?"

"For the liveliness of your mind, I did."

. . . "My resolution of thanking you for your kindness toward Lydia had certainly great effect. . ."

". . . Lady Catherine's unjustifiable endeavors to separate us were the means of removing all my doubts."

*The light of the eyes rejoices the heart,
and good news refreshes the bones.*
Proverbs 15:30

❧

When Darcy arrived with Bingley for that first visit, he was discouraged by Elizabeth's seeming lack of care for him. He saw her as silent and grave, giving him no encouragement of a hope of any further relationship between them. Elizabeth blamed her behavior on embarrassment.

But thankfully, two events brought about the needed catalyst for a renewed understanding between them: first was Lady Catherine's attempt at separating them; second was Elizabeth's deciding to thank Mr. Darcy for his role in Lydia's marriage. By Elizabeth refusing to submit to Lady Catherine's demand, she sent hope back to Darcy, through his aunt's account of her stubbornness. And when a time to walk alone presented itself, Elizabeth encouraged Darcy's heart by expressing gratitude for his generosity towards Lydia.

Our reactions, the welcoming or discouragement that emanates from our gaze, can be the trigger that strengthens or weakens a relationship. Elizabeth's original embarrassment, which caused gravity, alienated Mr. Darcy. But the report of her honest answer to Lady Catherine created the needed hope in his heart. May we nurture our ability to welcome and encourage by the warmth of greeting that is reflected in our eyes.

DAY ONE HUNDRED AND TWENTY

❧✦

Happy for all her maternal feelings was the day on which Mrs. Bennet got rid of her two most deserving daughters. . .

Mr. Bennet missed his second daughter exceedingly; his affection for her drew him oftener from home than anything else could do. He delighted in going to Pemberley, especially when he was least expected.

Mr. Bingley and Jane remained at Netherfield only a twelvemonth . . . The darling wish of his sisters was then gratified; he bought an estate in the neighboring county to Derbyshire and Jane and Elizabeth, in addition to every other source of happiness, were within thirty miles of each other.

Kitty, to her very material advantage, spent the chief of her time with her two elder sisters. In society so superior, her improvement was great. . .

Mary was the only daughter who remained at home; and she was necessarily drawn from the pursuit of accomplishments by Mrs. Bennet's being quite unable to sit alone. . .

As for Wickham and Lydia, their characters suffered no revolution from the marriage of her sisters.

Pemberley was now Georgiana's home; and the attachment of the sisters was exactly what Darcy had hoped to see.

With the Gardiners they were always on the most intimate terms. Darcy, as well as Elizabeth, really loved them; and they were both ever sensible of the warmest gratitude towards the persons who, by bringing her into Derbyshire, had been the means of uniting them.

Love is patient and kind; love does not envy or boast; it is not arrogant or rude. It does not insist on its own way; it is not irritable or resentful; it does not rejoice at wrongdoing, but rejoices with the truth. Love bears all things, believes all things, hopes all things, endures all things. Love never ends. As for prophecies, they will pass away; as for tongues, they will cease; as for knowledge, it will pass away.
I Corinthians 13:4-8

Mr. Darcy and Elizabeth's relationship began on the rockiest of all footings, but ended with mutual love, respect, and good will. Through humble transparency, they accepted their own faults, and changed, leading to a beautiful union.

True love, which is selfless and thoughtful of the other, never fails to produce a beautiful relationship between two people. The various aspects of love, practiced with a purpose, can heal wounds and unite hearts and souls. Love never fails.

Principles and Proverbs from Pride and Prejudice

Chrisann Dawson

ABOUT THE AUTHOR

Chrisann has been writing her whole life. As a child, she started hundreds of stories that she never finished.

She has taught high school English Grammar and Composition for more than twenty years and was blessed by the opportunity to teach English as a second language in the Congo, Africa through the Lingala language.

Chrisann is now finishing her stories. Lots of them. Shine-A-Light Press will be publishing her trilogy of novels inspired by her time in the Congo in 2021.

She has three adult children and currently lives in Northern Arizona with her husband, Gale.

www.ingramcontent.com/pod-product-compliance
Lightning Source LLC
Chambersburg PA
CBHW030433010526
44118CB00011B/621